bridgital nation

ADVANCE PRAISE FOR THE BOOK

'*Bridgital Nation* offers a penetrating look at today's India, and suggests a novel approach for reimagining automation as a human aid, not a replacement'—Satya Nadella, CEO, Microsoft

'*Bridgital Nation* is a beautifully written book, with its authentic view of India from the trenches coupled with an ambitious vision for the country. It brings to life the challenges of jobs and access to basic services like health and education through real-life narratives of people across India. This book shows how the deliberate use of AI and machine learning, coupled with human skills, can solve these issues and place India on an accelerated path to growth and prosperity. This book is a must-read for anyone who wants to understand today's India and how it could be a force to be reckoned with in the coming decade'—Indra Nooyi, former CEO, PepsiCo

'The economic challenges facing the world require us to bring people and technology together. Bridgital shows that with creative new approaches, success is possible'—Michael Bloomberg, CEO, Bloomberg L.P.

'An absolutely brilliant book, based on deep analysis and rooted in practical insights. N. Chandra and Roopa Purushothaman combine decades of experience of applying technology to problems at scale and macroeconomic development, respectively. Bridgital is an original idea, to simultaneously find a way for India to create jobs and also improve access to services, using the latest technology. This book is a must-read for those aspiring to solve India's seemingly intractable challenges, at speed and population scale'—Nandan Nilekani, co-founder and chairman, Infosys, and founding chairman, UIDAI (Aadhaar)

'Innovation focused on creating access and building markets has been the core of economic development for countries throughout the world, and India is no different. Chandra helped build one of

India's most innovative and successful companies, and so knows first-hand what creating this growth requires. What Chandra and Roopa propose in *Bridgital Nation* is an extremely insightful look at how India can harness technological innovation to transform its economy'—Clayton Christensen, professor of business administration, Harvard Business School

'*Bridgital Nation* is a brilliant book that should be mandatory reading for anyone interested in charting a new path forward for India in the twenty-first century. Through gripping ethnographic depictions and examples, N. Chandrasekaran and Roopa Purushothaman identify the unique circumstances of India's contemporary challenges in areas ranging from health care to job creation, and from education to entrepreneurship. But this book does not simply analyse problems: rather, it provides carefully considered proposals for moving forward with the urgency India requires. India's growing and young population—with all its problems of inadequate human capital, weak infrastructure and cultural conservatism—is seen as a tremendous resource: so long as new technological solutions are adapted to these conditions. Thus "digital" becomes "bridgital"—a precisely rendered set of accommodations and adaptations that use technology to supplement rather than substitute for human labour, extending both human capacity and the capacity of the nation to offer far more robust opportunities in education, healthcare, employment and social development'—Nicholas B. Dirks, former chancellor, University of California, Berkeley

'This is a fascinating and important book. The authors intelligently describe the pressing challenges that India faces but also the opportunities to overcome them provided by technology and smart policy. *Bridgital Nation* brings a scholarly attention to data and analysis as well as street smarts and common sense—a rare combination! I read it and found myself nodding in agreement and just hoping that India's leaders read it carefully'—Fareed Zakaria, journalist and host of CNN's Fareed Zakaria GPS

bridgital nation

SOLVING TECHNOLOGY'S PEOPLE PROBLEM

N. CHANDRASEKARAN
AND
ROOPA PURUSHOTHAMAN

Foreword by RATAN N. TATA

PENGUIN
ALLEN
LANE

An imprint of Penguin Random House

ALLEN LANE

USA | Canada | UK | Ireland | Australia
New Zealand | India | South Africa | China

Allen Lane is part of the Penguin Random House group of companies
whose addresses can be found at global.penguinrandomhouse.com

Published by Penguin Random House India Pvt. Ltd
4th Floor, Capital Tower 1, MG Road,
Gurugram 122 002, Haryana, India

First published in Allen Lane by Penguin Random House India 2019

ISBN 9780670093366

Typeset in Dante MT Std by Manipal Digital Systems, Manipal
Printed at Replika Press Pvt. Ltd.

www.penguin.co.in

For a country that cannot wait

Contents

Contents

Contents

Foreword

Ratan N. Tata

Technology is driving change around us at a terrific pace. The transformation to a digital world has had and will continue to have a profound impact on the way we live, work and learn. However, this global transformation is not always smooth and predictable, as it may not adequately allow for social factors or recognize the importance of a human interface.

Bridgital Nation addresses these issues in the context of India and emphasizes the need to build human bridges which recognize the diversity of the human interface with its varied educational base, skill sets and access to infrastructure. In the book, the authors demonstrate, through anecdotal examples, how such bridges can improve digital transformation by extending technology-aided capabilities and goals. The authors make a case for deconstructing and reimagining projects to more effectively enhance outputs and set goals, while conserving resources and harnessing available human capacity.

The book provides an interesting perspective on what might be an effective means of tapping the vast underutilized human resource base which exists in India. It advocates three transformational requirements—Technology, Talent and Vision—as important foundations to help solve people's problems with major technological transformation.

Bridgital Nation tackles the strategic options available for a country to truly develop in a world driven and shaped by technological change. It shows how technology can create a pathway for government, businesses, regulators, NGOs and everyday people to close the gaps that matter most. It provides a thoughtful balance using available technology and available human resources to make a success of the transformation into the digital world of tomorrow.

19 September 2019
Mumbai

Introduction

During the first days of India's smart city initiative in 2015, MyGov.in, a government website, asked Indians to imagine what a smart city transformation would look like. The response was enthusiastic. There were hundreds of suggestions to use technology in ingenious ways, of course. Still, scrolling down the pages, it was clear that a much larger number were interested in getting what they already had to work properly. They suggested that smart cities should have running water, uninterrupted power, and trucks that picked up garbage twice a day. A truly smart city, they said, would have streetlights that worked at night.

The city they described—the city of their imagination— was nothing more than a functional city.

Picture, for a moment, the same survey on a larger scale: If citizens had to imagine not a smart city but a smart nation, the range of their concerns would significantly expand.

They would desire better healthcare and jobs. Mobility. Security. Quicker justice. Fewer regulations. The concerns of life. Yet India, which has known of these challenges for decades, has struggled to provide its people what they need. And now time, which once seemed an infinite resource, has begun to grow scarce. There are more Indians jostling for the same resources with every passing month, and at the other end, technology's transformations are on the horizon. There is a narrow window to realize the potential of India's demographic endowments.

This book started out as an attempt to understand how technology could help India navigate this crucial transition period. It soon became apparent that there were two primary challenges that needed urgent attention: Jobs, and access to vital services. Whether in education, healthcare, the judiciary, or any other field, the problems remain the same—both resources and skilled people are scarce.

India will have to think about its problems in new ways, because the old ideas have proven unsuccessful time and again. In the twenty-first century, these new ways need to harness the power of artificial intelligence (AI), the cloud, machine learning and the Internet of Things (IoT), considering the rate at which they are expanding what is possible on a daily basis. The combination of these technologies can provide answers to problems that just a few years ago may have been considered intractable. However, the approach to technology requires careful consideration. It means not being distracted by the array of possibilities, or simply mimicking the innovations of others, but being razor-focused on what is needed. Not technology for technology's sake, but technology in context—applied in ways that make sense to people, and that can help increase the yield of India's existing human and physical resources.

This lies at the heart of our book's argument: The future, if India is to harness it, has to come from a mutually beneficial relationship between its citizens and new applications of technology. Neither human nor machine alone can help India prepare for the great changes at its doorstep.

This contrasts the dominant portrayal of the future that, in economic and imaginative terms, is typically seen through the lens of developed economies. For decades, we have heard in general terms that robots are coming for jobs, for the future, and for all of us. As early as in 1964, a memo sent to the president of the United States envisioned a 'cybernation revolution' which would result in 'a system of almost unlimited productive capacity' that would replace human labour.[1]

Since then, the questions and concerns have become more specific. How will the advent of machines affect jobs? What jobs will be the first to go? What will it mean for the way we work, live and play? The conversation is accompanied by video footage that seems to confirm our worst fears: We see machines in a sterile warehouse sort packages before they are sent; we see the skeletal frame of a headless metal bot run, leap over obstacles, jog on snow, stagger but not fall after being pushed, and right itself if it falls over. We see more reliable models of ourselves.

The other view is more pragmatic. When new orders emerge, there are societal leaps in productivity, jobs, and living standards. Jobs will be lost, but others will be created. Over 120 years ago, even before the start of Ford's automobile assembly line, it was evident that horse carriages were on their way out. '[The] time is coming when the vehicle drawn by horses will be the one to excite remark, and the present novelty will be a thing of ordinary use,' a reader wrote to the *New York Times* in 1899.[2] When costs fell and the market for 'horseless carriages' grew, new technologies and jobs emerged at fuel stations, repair shops, and automobile dealerships. History shows us that these economic and technology-led transitions inspire feelings of discomfort and uncertainty. Now, as then, these views often look at a future without automation and a future with automation, not an in-between future where both coexist.

Imagining where AI and automation, the main drivers of the Fourth Industrial Revolution,[3] will end up is certainly an enticing and terrifying exercise. But what keeps governments and leaders awake at night is not its final form. It is what will come before that—the inevitable social, political and business costs that will only gradually become clear. They understand, deep in their bones, that this time truly is different. Automation in the past focused on repetitive tasks, done by hand and on foot. Now, tasks of cognition—thinking itself—are the objects of automation.

But, as the physicist Michio Kaku says about general cognitive ability—common sense, by another name—even the most advanced robots and algorithms today have the intelligence of a cockroach.[4] We have time.

What we need is a new approach that views AI and automation as a human aid, not a replacement for human intervention. If we do this, automation in India will look nothing like it does anywhere else. We call this approach 'Bridgital'.

First, though, we have to understand India.

A Reluctant Subject

A book about India is a book about an inscrutable place. There is the everyday country of the senses, and then the country made of numbers—the analyst's country. One is overwhelming, the other is confounding. It's a rare day when their stories line up.

The India of the senses tells us about the challenges its citizens witness every day. Indians see them in moments—the crowded clinics, the bustling courts—without recognizing that disparate issues are closely connected. These moments can stretch into years—the desire to work but not the opportunity, the absence of professional care for children and elders. The influences these issues bear are subtle. In quiet ways, they affect how Indians seek health and employment, and affect how their children think.

But numbers are what anchor our understanding of a country's trajectory, and the first numbers we see tell us that progress and prosperity are imminent.

In a few grains of sand, India's ranks will swell to 1.5 billion. Over 700 million Indians are below the age of thirty—more than twice the size of the entire population of the United States. Every month, on average, a million more Indians become of working age.[5] The country's GDP per capita is ₹140,000 ($2,000) right now, but will more than double to around ₹300,000 ($4,300) in a decade. By 2030, India will become the world's third-largest economy. This period will be marked by rising household aspirations, increased formalization of the economy, and widespread digital maturity. By 2050, India's GDP per capita could rise to ₹1.1 million ($15,000).[6]

While the glide-path to greater prosperity sounds smooth and inevitable, India rarely lives in its averages. A far more complex and fascinating story is playing out on the ground.

India's distinct cultural histories, languages, and governance mean that individual states operate like thirty or more discrete entities that rarely reflect the national average.[7] So while the nation's income per capita is ₹140,000 ($2,000), annual income in Delhi and Goa is around ₹350,000 ($5,000)—similar to the global median. Meanwhile, at less than ₹42,000 ($600), Bihar's income per capita is in the bottom decile globally.[8]

The state of Uttar Pradesh alone has more people than Brazil. Maharashtra's population is larger than Germany's. Ten states account for most of the value of the country's goods and services. Two-thirds of all manufacturing occurs in seven states. Just five states are responsible for over half of all postgraduates.[9] India's rural and urban markets often pull in different directions at the same time, with one growing while the other slows.

These differences magnify the perils of a broad brush.

Partly, India is hard to pin down because of its idiosyncrasies. The country's wide and complex spectrum of realities has been historically micromanaged by a sweeping, risk-averse bureaucracy (for instance, until recently, there used to be rules limiting what products enterprises of a certain size could manufacture). Even as GDP growth has averaged over 7 per cent a year for the past decade, a surprisingly large number of women have left the workforce. For all the excitement around India's start-up culture, the country's average firm employs just over two people.[10] Domestic markets dominate India's economy, in contrast to China, South Korea and Thailand.

The other part is down to timing. India's development has come in an era of globalization and technology-driven change, processes that the country has at times embraced, and at times turned away from. Economic growth is driven by the services sector—information technology, finance, telecommunications—rather than the manufacturing-led progress seen historically across the rest of Asia. There are other incongruities. Households purchase televisions and mobile phones before they reach basic nutrition levels. The country has successfully attempted some of the world's most ambitious technological programmes (Aadhaar,[11] for example), yet its levels of child malnutrition are still daunting.[12]

Why does this matter? By 2050, as the world's third-largest economy, India will have a per capita income of ₹1.1 million ($15,000). Meanwhile, as the second-largest, the US will have an income per capita of roughly ₹7 million ($100,000). Behind India will be Japan as the world's fourth-largest economy, with a per capita income of ₹5.3 million ($76,000).[13] What will it mean for India to carry the mantle of a global economic powerhouse while its citizens struggle with the bare essentials of a middle-class lifestyle? How will this dynamic affect the compromises India will have to make when it comes to questions of, say, trade or pollution? India's rise on the global stage means that the largest economies in the world (in terms of GDP) will no longer be the richest.[14] This sounds simple, but its implications for geopolitical alignment and strategic priorities among the world's major economies will be significant—and may already be influencing the backlash to globalization we see across the world today.

In other words, as India grows into the third-largest economy over the next decade, housing one-fourth of the global middle class, a significant share of its population will still be at the bottom of the pyramid.[15] The rift between the India of numbers and senses, between averages and lived experience, will still be far from bridged.

What holds India back from reaching its full potential? The issues have a name. We call them 'India's Twin Challenges': Jobs and Access.

JOBS

India has a massive jobs challenge on its hands. Ninety million people will come of working age between 2020 and 2030—a continent's worth of eager, ambitious, energetic young jobseekers. The promise of these numbers is breathtaking, especially when they are set against other large economies. In the same period, the number of Indians reaching working age will be four times that of the US, Brazil and Indonesia combined.

When they arrive, they will find an economy that is growing, but is low on gainful work opportunities. Given the lack of reliable data, estimates about the number of jobs created in recent years range from as many as 15 million jobs added in a year, to millions of jobs actually being lost. These estimates provide glimpses into parts of the economy, but never the whole picture.

The entrants who eventually find work—overall, the unemployment rate is 6 per cent[16]—will by and large feel disappointed by the story they have been sold. Most of them will join the informal sector, where there is no shortage of work, but where low productivity, low wages, and the absence of job security and safety are rife.[17] Informal sector jobs often fail to meet even the lowest bar of a good job.

Good Jobs, According to the Good Jobs Institute at MIT[18]

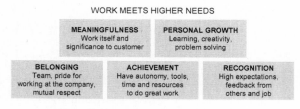

Source: The Good Jobs Institute

India's particular challenge is that a very large number of working-age adults—many of whom are not even in the labour force at this time—need to find productive jobs that they can perform at their existing levels of skill and education. About 66 per cent of the workforce have, at best, the equivalent of an eighth-grade education. Only around one in fifty workers have any kind of formal vocational training.[19] Making matters more acute, sectors of the economy that provide productive jobs—like manufacturing and services—use educated and skilled workers to a greater degree than would be expected.

The result is a visible split in the nature of the Indian economy—a high-skill, high-productivity sector that produces goods and services for wealthy, tech-savvy, and urban consumers alongside external markets, and a low-cost, low-productivity sector that is mostly geared towards the poor. India is missing a 'middle'—the midway jobs, the mid-skilled workers.

Put simply, India is at the leading edge of the question of what happens when a sizeable portion of humanity struggles to find gainful employment.

ACCESS

Jobs are only one half of the problem. The other is a critical shortage in access to vital services. We may not know it by

name, but we are living witnesses to the access challenge—
the village healer offering miraculous treatments on a bicycle;
the tired driver who drove his truck into a highway ditch;
the overcrowded classrooms and doctors' waiting rooms
with no place to sit; the legal case that goes on for decades;
the countless middlemen and agencies that help make sense
of it all.

The access challenge puts services such as quality health
and education out of reach for millions of Indians[20]—a
situation that has arisen in large part because there aren't
enough qualified people.

For example, it will take a further 600,000 doctors
and 2.5 million nurses, a million teachers, about 400,000
agricultural extension workers, and 1.7 million commercial
vehicle drivers to meet India's current needs.[21] Despite the
30 million cases pending within India's judicial system, the
country has only three quarters of the judges it needs.[22]
There aren't enough researchers, plumbers or welders
either. The list is a long one because the shortages are
endemic. With each passing year, the shortfall is felt a
little more, because more people are jostling for the same
limited resources.

The access challenge has other costs. People travel
extraordinarily long distances to seek basic services, often
at high cost to themselves. This leads to overcrowding in
classes, clinics, courtrooms, and everywhere else. Inevitably,

quality declines, because specialists are unable to meet the demand for their knowledge and services, and can't spend enough time on their patients, students, cases or customers.

Addressing this challenge will bear fruit almost immediately. It will mean shorter wait times. It will mean faster justice. It will mean better quality healthcare and education. It will make people feel less like a crowd, more like they matter. It will improve the quality of life.

•—•

India has an overwhelming demand for vital services, and an overwhelming supply of human capital. It just doesn't know how to build a bridge between them.

This is likely because India has never asked itself how they could converge. Instead, the question about jobs has focused on how jobs can be created. Thinking about employment this way has led India down the well-worn path of turning to existing industries that drive economic growth, and adjusting regulations, like fine-tuning a radio. In one year, India encourages the garment and textile manufacturing industry. In another, it gives the film industry a 'single window clearance'.[23]

Yet these are, at best, partial answers. India struggles because the sectors of its economy that are growing the fastest are not employment intensive. What's needed is a bridge that allows industries and people to step up and move closer to the formal, more productive end of the economy. This can be done by improving the quality of jobs and helping workers achieve higher skill levels, while simultaneously creating an environment in which firms of all sizes can drive formal job growth.

In other words, India can no longer tinker at the margins of the twin challenges. What's required is a complete reimagining of how its parts work.

Bridgital Nation

This is where technology, in context, enters the picture. Bridgital holds the key to pulling India out of this conundrum. It works with the novel understanding that the two challenges go hand in hand. By turning a challenge into an opportunity—seeing India's access challenge as an engine of employment generation—it builds a technology-based bridge between the dual parts of the Indian economy. It helps build the 'middle' that India sorely needs.

The Bridgital approach is a simple one. Technology is there to amplify India's existing resources and extend them to many more Indians. Bridgital does this by reimagining how services can be delivered and how people can use their talents differently, once they are aided by technology. By using AI, machine learning, IoT and the cloud in a deliberate way, it can help people access services while, at the same time, providing gainful work. But technology alone isn't the answer; it has to be configured and adapted to the demands of the situation. Bridgital works best when roles and services are deconstructed and reimagined, and when the delivery of the tasks they contain is redesigned.

In the Bridgital world, technology does not disrupt an existing market as much as it creates an entirely new one. With that comes a fundamental layer of jobs—both direct and indirect—that support the successful delivery of services like healthcare and education. When services are reimagined through twenty-first-century technological advances, an additional layer of workers emerge who can intermediate both technology and existing resources for larger numbers of people.

Workers augmented by technology take on tasks previously done only by experts and specialists. There is also demand for people who can act as tech-enabled intermediaries between those who need services and those who supply them—demand that, today, is often serviced by the informal sector. Workers in these roles are up-skilled, up-qualified and made comfortable with technology designed to aid their work. This frees up time for specialized workers to focus on the most vital tasks they could be performing, such as serving more people. The result is a more inclusive, productive and formalized system.

This can be a gift that keeps on giving. Freedom from disease and despair, lower transaction costs, access to better education, a better quality of life, will all unleash the creative and productive potential of India's people and improve the employability of workers over the long run. The more access India creates, the more jobs it will make available to its people, setting off a virtuous cycle of inclusion and growth. Bridgital thinking uses technology as an enabler, a tool, to make the most of what India has, and give the country what it most needs.

This is the kind of thinking India needs more of: Innovation that addresses the country's persistent resource deficits in ways unimaginable in the past; and that enhances its workers, rather than replaces them. Throughout this book, we show how this can play out in health, education, agriculture, financial services and logistics. If this strategy is realized, the digital transformation India will undergo can take a form unlike in any other country. Done well, it could positively impact 30 million jobs by 2025 and lead to a 10-20 per cent increase in wages for workers, while giving over 200 million citizens access to better services including health and education.[24]

The future will be one of humans and technology working together. It's this future India will have to anticipate and design for, keeping its young workforce, limited infrastructure, and linguistic and cultural differences in mind.

• — •

In tackling the twin challenges at the scale India requires, two other strategies stand out. These two strategies address jobs and access, while complementing the Bridgital approach.

1) The XX Factor: Bringing women to the workforce.

Under a quarter of women in India engage in paid work. This measure is low in comparison to other countries at similar income levels, and surprisingly, it has fallen in the past decade. Nearly 120 million Indian women—more than double the entire population of South Korea—have at least a secondary education, but do not participate in the workforce.

The XX Factor[25] addresses the jobs challenge by allowing more of India's secondary-educated population to transition into the jobs market. For a country that urgently needs skilled workers, their absence is deeply felt in the labour force. If even half of this group of women entered the workforce, in one stroke, the share of workers with at least a secondary education would jump from 33 per cent to 46 per cent—the equivalent of fifteen years' worth of improvement. This alone could add ₹31 trillion ($440 billion) to India's GDP.[26]

Women will form an important part of the pool of Bridgital workers. What will it take to bring them to work? Smart policies focused on childcare provision and parental leave, and promoting attitudinal shifts in society around working women are good places to begin. The last decade of experience and research has brought this opportunity to light. India now needs to shift gears and understand better how to make paid work available to and worthwhile for women. With a more balanced educational profile, the country can address a key part of the skills gap it faces. For this to take place, the access barriers to women's employment need a serious overhaul.

2) Entrepreneurs everywhere: Preparing the ground for thriving entrepreneurship throughout the country.

When it comes to jobs, the country has to think hard about both the nature and size of its firms. The Indian business landscape is characterized by a large number of micro businesses, many of which are simply self-employed individuals who are optimistically called 'entrepreneurs'.

They aren't. What they run are survival ventures, the only road available, the last throw of the dice. If they had a choice, many of these 'entrepreneurs' would probably opt for staid, unglamorous salaried jobs.

In most economies, the engines of job growth are small and medium enterprises (SMEs), which tend to employ between ten and 250 workers each. These businesses provide services locally—think of local hotels, restaurants, health clinics, salons and so on. Across developing countries, SMEs account for over a third of private sector employment; in India, the figure stands at just above a tenth.[27]

A new focus on entrepreneurship throughout the country—bringing India to developing-country averages—could potentially shift 45 million workers into more productive employment in small and medium enterprises.[28] These jobs are more formal, and pay better wages than the opportunities on offer for most job seekers today. Everywhere entrepreneurship can flourish through the development of Bridgital clusters that integrate and extend a range of digital business services, which many SMEs lack access to. Bridgital clusters, coupled with the deeper use of digital governance to transform the relationship between SMEs and the bureaucracy, can positively channel the entrepreneurial spirit inherent throughout the nation.

These strategies are deeply interwoven. Bridgital provides the unprecedented 'bridge' between jobs and access, while XX Factor and Everywhere Entrepreneurship bolster both sides of the scale—multiplying the impact on jobs and access. India needs to solve the twin challenges for hundreds of millions, but the beauty of a technology-driven approach is that scale can take hold.

Bridgital will provide new opportunities to meet the needs of small and medium businesses. The deconstruction and reimagining of how services are delivered will create new markets and provide new business opportunities for them. One of the biggest hurdles that many small and medium businesses face is in finding skilled workers. And even if they find skilled workers, because there are so few of them, they cannot afford them. Bridgital expands the pool of skilled workers through the aid of technology. Bridgital clusters can also extend tools and technologies that make it easier to find these workers. Similarly, given the high levels of informality in India's economy, a combination of the Bridgital transformation of industries and thriving everywhere entrepreneurship can provide a meaningful route to paid work for women.

A common train of thought connects these strategies— an attempt to pull together what India's unique development journey has, so far, pushed apart.

•—•

Introduction

There's a word in Sanskrit—*antarlaapika*. It means a puzzle or a riddle in which the answer is hidden within the riddle itself. India is an *antarlaapika* that can be solved with three strategies from within. Each of the three strategies we identified involves interrogating a host of deep-rooted beliefs. These are decidedly not quick fixes. However, they need to be seen as part of the solution to the country's twin challenges, not simply as issues in isolation. We don't have to look at digital approaches as simply cost-cutting, profit-enhancing exercises. They can augment our human capital, if we choose wisely. We don't have to look at gender as solely an inclusion issue. It is firmly a talent decision. We don't have to look at entrepreneurship with the singular lens of creating billion-dollar unicorns. It is a strength that we can leverage throughout the country. These are all critical bridges to a better future of work for India.

Envisioning a different future is easy; it is vastly more challenging to bring these visions into the real world, while correcting the errors of the past and reassessing our approach to doing things going forward. To build a new kind of country and take it into the future, it is often assumed, requires a large budget and new plans that capture the popular imagination. But the problem with such an approach is its focus on newness, not outcomes, as the guiding principle. This kind of thinking leads to new technologies being heralded as saviours. It sends us on hospital- and school-building sprees, while neglecting what has already been made at great cost.

In truth, we already have what it takes to create more and better jobs. We also have the capability to improve and make better use of the existing skill levels of our people, especially once we tailor digital approaches and technologies to our needs. What if doctors, perennially in short supply, were able to treat more patients once their administrative duties were reduced? What if reassigning those duties created new jobs and a new class of worker? What if that class of worker was aided by technology? What if we stopped thinking of humans and technology as competing for the same work?

This book is a portrait of a most reluctant subject and its citizens. A part of it describes how the challenges of jobs and access keep millions of Indians from offering their best. But it also shows how three clearly defined strategies can hit at the root of the problems that hold India back. We look to rich examples of success, within India and across other countries, that can be replicated or at least, hold universal lessons.

We draw on our experience working in the Tata Group, as well as the Group's 150-year history and work across India.[29] This puts us in a unique position to witness the unprecedented and layered set of challenges India faces. We see ourselves sitting amongst these issues: Struggling with gender representation, with making workspaces safer, becoming digitally agile. This book is a part of our own ongoing attempts to learn and figure out next steps.

But this book is more than that alone. It's about the gaps that turn ordinary things into extraordinary tasks, and about the people forced to be extraordinary to bridge those gaps. Within it, you will find remarkable human stories that celebrate the resilience, grit, and ingenuity of Indians going about their lives despite the obstacles they face every day. With this work, our aim is to go beyond averages and sweeping statistics and help foster a deeper understanding of India and the needs of Indians by telling you about their lives. It is our attempt at bridging the India of the numbers with the India of the senses.

The Bridgital Transformation

1

Flashing Lights

Nikhil Burman parked his car beside National Highway 37 in Silchar, Assam, turned on the hazard lights, and waited in the darkness. The blinking lights were for the people coming down from distant towns and villages few people could find on a map. He could not see them, but wanted them to see him; they were coming for him.

While he waited, same as every night at 8.30, a crowd grew around the car. Older women, young men and women, people of all ages, all thrust their papers and their questions at him. His phones rang endlessly. Arriving trains brought more people and more questions.

His visitors came because they were sick, and deeply in need of anyone who could help. Someone—a friend or relative in their village—had told them of a man who parked his car beside the highway, turned on the flashing lights, and answered questions. That was what brought them out of the hills, across living root bridges a hundred years old, down mountain roads that ran along ravines, and across state lines: Someone who could guide them to the right doctor.

The surprise was that Nikhil was a driver, and had no medical training at all. His expertise was in helping patients go where they needed to be. Few patients asked him about his qualifications. He seemed to know what he was doing.

He listened patiently to one caller's lengthy list of complaints, noting them down on his other phone, an old piece that had a chipped screen and was worn at the edges. He composed reminders to himself on SMS, typing the patient's name and a code for which test had to be done: SABITA BHOWMIK GC, or RAJIB DAS SKD. He told the caller to not eat because the tests he needed required an empty stomach. Nikhil could not discuss the particulars of the caller's ailments, but assured him that he would arrange the pickup from Silchar railway station, appointments with doctors, examinations and tests, and even a place to stay. Nikhil was nearly forty, but looked a decade younger. It was his manner—firm, business-like, reassuring—that gave strangers confidence.

A man stepped out of a rickshaw and walked over to Nikhil. He introduced himself, handed over some papers and, without being asked, bowed to present his head. Nikhil assessed the nature of the lump on the man's skull with two fingers, like a doctor would. In less than a minute, he concluded which doctor the man had to see. An elderly villager walked up. She was tired, with worry written over her face. This was her first time outside her village. This was the first time she had been so sick. Her stomach hurt, and no one in the village knew what to do. Someone told her about a driver who could lead her to the right treatment, and gave her Nikhil's number. Now she found herself, a nine-hour train journey later, on a dark highway, in front of a complete stranger, handing over her medical file.

Nikhil found the woman a place to stay, and prepared her for what would come next. He told her they would drive to Kalyani Hospital the next day, consult doctors, and do some tests. He explained that an operation could follow. The woman listened, but could not stop worrying. She was all alone. To reassure her, Nikhil told her he would buy her medicines from a pharmacy, and take care of any other formalities associated with the surgery.

'But if you die here,' he remembered to tell her, 'I will not send your body back to Tripura. I will arrange for you to be cremated here. Understood?'

In the end, it was a simple procedure to remove a few kidney stones. No complications. Still, Nikhil had worked with patients for a long time. She was older, and he didn't want to take any chances.

2

Playing Roles

Each evening, Nikhil met with dozens of patients to help them understand what to expect from their visit to Silchar's hospitals and clinics. On any given day, he estimated, there were usually over two hundred calls from patients in Tripura.[1]

Nikhil's 'career' as a full-time medical coordinator came about entirely by accident. In 2000, soon after he finished school, he began shuttling passengers across Silchar in his father's auto-rickshaw. One of his frequent customers, a senior doctor at a charitable hospital in the town, found him dependable enough to ask a question: Would Nikhil like to transport patients between the places where they were receiving medical treatment?

Nikhil agreed.

Before long, he began to view life through patients' eyes. Most patients required active help on their arrival in Silchar, having only heard of the place. They arrived bewildered and clutching their medical files, not on a professional's advice, but on the recommendation of a friend, family member, or neighbour. This meant that few doctors were referring patients to specialists, which, in turn, meant that patients spent time trying to find the right doctor all by themselves. They wandered out of consultations and surgeries, wondering what to do next. They all seemed lost and uneasy this far from home, in an unfamiliar and imposing town that bustled with noise, energy and action.

Once they did find a doctor, there was the small matter that doctors and patients spoke different languages. Nikhil saw doctors speak in their second or third language to a nurse, who then struggled to translate complex diagnoses and prognoses to patients in a regional dialect. One could only guess how much was lost in translation.

Nikhil sensed the deep suspicion with which rural patients approached doctors in large hospitals. Beyond the question of whether patients would comply with instructions they only partially understood, he observed a deeper disconnect—of which differences in language was only the most apparent part. It was human nature to be less trusting in a foreign environment, especially if the diagnosis was of life-altering significance.

When people travelled a long way for medical treatment, the problem was probably a serious one, something that did not have a simple cure. But the shock of a diagnosis was often so great that they refused to trust anything doctors said, and refused to act on medical advice until it was too late. Most had never undergone diagnostic tests, and never been required to understand what reports said. Besides, they were preoccupied with the more mundane concerns: An affordable place to stay in town, transportation, medicine, appointments.

Nurses and doctors were ready to help, of course, but there were endless lines of patients and not enough healthcare providers. They were already doing all kinds of work to keep the hospitals running. Doctors administered injections that nurses otherwise would, and nurses filed documents, made funeral arrangements, and did paperwork for government schemes. Witnessing all this, Nikhil realized that patients longed for guidance from someone who felt friendly and familiar. Someone who could coax and cajole them, as a youth from their village might; someone who could simplify the process of seeking help and alleviate the helplessness they felt.

The entire edifice of healthcare relies on creating an environment of trust, yet trust was in short supply. Nikhil saw the role he could play. 'Patients come here thinking they know what ails them and what they might need to do,' he said. 'When they receive a different diagnosis, they get overwhelmed. They need guidance, and need to hear their options carefully explained. Navigating the medical system itself should be the least of their problems.'

Nikhil saw himself primarily as a logistics manager; but while he was careful not to give medical advice, he frequently ended up as a de facto triage nurse, directing patients to certain facilities based on his past experience with cases like theirs. He charged a minuscule daily amount for his services, and fully expected to be haggled down. Several patients needed discounts, and one in five was too poor to pay at all. If someone could not afford even the bargained-down price, Nikhil waived his fee.

Demand continued to grow, and providing guidance became a full-time business. His fleet of cars grew to seven vehicles. His relatives joined the business, doing what he did. But Nikhil was in it through and through. On occasion, he paused work to donate blood to a customer.

Seen one way, Nikhil was an entrepreneur, ingenious in finding and serving a market. Across Silchar, their lights blinking in the night, other drivers played a similar role.

But seen another way, if India's systems worked the way they were intended, this market would not exist at all.

3

Wrapping Technology around People

Indians go to spectacular lengths for the most basic things. The graduates who join millions to apply for a few dozen entry-level positions. The rural traveller undertaking an epic journey from home to see a doctor while she worries about her work, her money, her family. When an endeavour is successful, the effort it takes is forgotten. The enormous odds, once they are overcome, gradually seem less daunting. But this success is also a sign of deficiency. Unexceptional tasks are made exceptional only by the difficulty in achieving them.

We believe there's a way to make things easier.

Using technology the right way, with targeted interventions, India can remove long-standing access barriers to vital services. Bridgital wraps technological advances around India's most abundant resource, its people, to multiply their capabilities and change how they work.

When we think about the future of technology and work, there are three important distinctions that set India apart from advanced economies, and that make Bridgital a significant opportunity for the country.

First, India's lack of markets means access will take precedence over efficiency.

Advanced economies have a host of mature markets in which digital transformation is focused on increasing efficiency. India doesn't lack efficient markets, it lacks markets themselves. In the absence of these outlets, people fill in and operate independently—sometimes at the very edge of the law—meeting the unfulfilled demand for healthcare or other basic goods and services.

This absence of mature markets is evident in financial services. Despite the success of the historic Jan Dhan Yojana, India's ambitious financial inclusion programme that increased bank account penetration from about 50 per cent to 80 per cent in just three years, there is still work to be done. The country has around 190 million adults without a bank account, making it the world's second-largest unbanked population after China. Of those who have a bank account, almost half did not use it in 2017, preferring to use cash for spending and saving.[1] New-age financial technology companies are already stepping in with data- and technology-led approaches to meet the demands of the underserved. For example, low-income entrepreneurs, who had never been able to access capital from banks, can do so as companies use analytics to assess their trustworthiness, reducing reliance on collateral and credit scores.

Building entirely new markets is a different beast to optimizing existing ones. It means prioritizing access, alongside efficiency. Technology adoption will create new markets within the Indian economy. As they are created, and entirely new ecosystems begin to form and spread, there will be demand for people skilled in the ways of these new technologies.

We believe that Bridgital workers—digitally literate and intermediately skilled workers whose capabilities are complemented by technology—can play a pivotal role in traversing the barriers that have prevented markets from developing. This is an opportunity to create a new category of worker who acts as a bridge, a guide, and a translator. As with cars, planes and computers, where new markets develop, new ecosystems flourish around them. For example, these ecosystems have already grown around the mobile revolution in Africa: Kenya's largest mobile operator directly employs only around 5,500 people, but has spurred the creation of over 130,000 mobile money outlets to handle the country's transition from cash to mobile money.[2]

Second, India faces a perennially limited supply of skilled human resources and physical assets.

It is widely known that India does not have enough skilled resources and expertise. Accompanying this is a lack of infrastructure and physical resources as well. India has only half the number of doctors recommended by the World Health Organisation. The availability of hospital beds is even more problematic, with around two-thirds fewer beds than the global average. A citizen in rural India experiences even greater deprivation than the overall figure suggests, because resources tend to agglomerate in large cities. More than 60 per cent of hospitals are in urban India, where only about a third of India resides. With a population of 1.3 billion and growing, India does not have enough physical infrastructure—hospitals, roads, schools, warehouses, testing centres—to match the challenges posed by its scale.[3]

India is making gains on these metrics, but will continue to be a stretched society. It will need to make the most of what resources it does have, through a combination of both people and technology.

Third, India's demographics demand a different approach to automation and AI.

Developed economies are well into middle age. China and the US will have a median age over thirty-eight by 2020 (Japan's will be over forty-eight).[4] The older that countries get, the fewer workers they have available. This shortage drives them to develop technologies that can substitute for labour. As ageing economies have automated, they have transformed production practices, making them leaner and more efficient. The choices they've made are about efficiency, a response to their particular concerns.

In contrast, the median age of India's population will be twenty-eight by 2020, and thirty-one by 2030. The problem India has is not of age or numbers; it is skills and qualifications. Therefore, India's approach to automation has to be distinct from China, the US and Japan; it has to focus on technologies that augment and raise people's skills.

India will not be able to simply cut and paste China's (and much of Asia's) development path. It will need to forge a new path and bring the twentieth-century growth model of manufacturing-led development into the twenty-first century. This new growth model requires an alternative strategy: Boosting a range of labour-intensive, intermediate economic activities that take care of India's vast unmet demand and shift people towards more formal characteristics of work. Bridgital is a way of doing just this.

•——•

In the early 1980s, there was no playbook for what came to be known as outsourcing. Tata Consultancy Services (TCS), India's first IT services firm, was then a far smaller organization. It had to convince hesitant clients that India had the brightest engineers, and that they could meet every business demand. Back then, it was common for representatives of large US and European companies to attend meetings, listen attentively, and politely decline to have a part of their work handled thousands of kilometres away. At one meeting, the head of a credit card company listened to a visiting TCS team distractedly, and then, at the end of the meeting, said, 'I don't believe you guys can do it. I'm not risking it. This has never been tested.' To this, the leader of the TCS contingent replied, 'I hope you will call me back.'

Within months, the company head called back. In a short while, other calls followed: From the city of Detroit for software for its police force, from a company in New York that wanted its banking software serviced, from Phoenix, Sydney, Venezuela. They were all participants in the Third Industrial Revolution, a period marked by the proliferation of computers and the development of information technology. It eventually led to the adoption of business models like global supply chains and business process outsourcing that are commonplace today, but were unthinkable at the time.

Technology's upheavals are constant, however, and no sooner was the third over than the Fourth Industrial

Revolution began. Even so, keeping an eye on the future requires learning from the past. Three key lessons, learned from building lasting businesses that ride the waves of technology's disruptions, serve us well when thinking about Bridgital.

The first lesson: Technology alone does not solve difficult problems. But when technology is applied in context with reimagined processes, the results can be magical.

Consider the case of electricity. When this new stream of power started to replace the steam engine and water wheels as the primary source of energy, the first twenty years (up to 1920) registered just small improvements in productivity. It was only between 1920 and 1935, when businesses changed to take advantage of the new technology, that factories achieved an immense growth in productivity.[5] Before electricity, factories were designed around the constraints of the single, fixed, power source, which dictated where immovable machines would be placed. There wasn't much choice. The product of those machines—half-finished articles—were wheeled around the factory and moved from machine to machine.

Electricity, with its ease of distribution, allowed for a more logical arrangement of machines, making the process faster, more efficient, and reducing waste. In the final calculation, the indirect gains from changing factory processes far outweighed the direct benefit of the lower energy costs electricity offered.

Still, technology alone tempts us time and again, and so solutions to pressing problems are seen only in technological terms. This explains why India has no dearth of advocates for 'stacks' and platforms for agriculture, education, the judiciary, and health. Yet applied in isolation, technological solutions can end up wasting time and money.

The husks of digital-only thinking are all around us. One of the more well-known examples is the Aakash tablet programme, whose objective was to make education accessible to over five million students by digitizing content and making it freely available on low-cost tablets. The ambition was there, the foundation wasn't; an initial trial revealed issues with the device's battery, screen and sound. The programme focused too heavily on developing an affordable device, and not enough on the content or how a tablet could change students' educational experience. Nor was there any clarity on which textbooks would be digitized. In class, teachers shunned the device. Aakash ended up being just a low-cost device that could run a few apps and handle a few different file formats. The programme was shut down in March 2015, having fallen short of its laudable intentions: 'What really crippled the programme was not the operational delays or logistical failures, but the . . . assumption that placing a tablet in a

41

student's hands would solve everything,' a critic of the programme wrote. 'What the tablets would ultimately do was become, for those who couldn't afford to maintain and use them, a burden.'[6]

This is technology's great trap. By failing to understand context, we end up with incredibly dazzling technology answers for the completely wrong question. We need to keep this in mind when deploying Fourth Industrial Revolution technologies in the real world: Reimagining processes can deliver much greater value than the direct gains afforded by new technology.

The second lesson comes from the learnings in our work that there is no such thing as 'purely digital' or 'purely physical'. All digital solutions interact with and add value to the physical world. We need to maintain an integrated physical–digital perspective, asking how these two realms can complement, rather than substitute for, each other.

This is playing out most starkly in modern retail, where key players from mass market to niche, large incumbents to small upstarts, are all shifting to a seamless multi-channel experience for customers. Online retailers, from the US to China, are increasingly realizing the value of a physical space where customers can experience products. Conversely, incumbent retailers with physical stores realize the value, convenience and efficiencies of an online digital-assist to the customer, whose buying journey increasingly demands the flexibility of this dual approach.

Meanwhile, physical infrastructure will benefit from incorporating digital interfaces and sensors. Everything from oil rigs to farm crops are being integrated into the Internet of Things—machines that 'talk' to each other on different kinds of networks. This will inevitably translate to more efficient resource usage in the physical world. Take the case of 'smart farming', where GPS data, soil scanning data and other bits of information can be used to make micro-level decisions about fertilizer and pesticide use. These can even take into account variations across the same farm, greatly improving yields and optimizing the use of inputs.

Pitting technology against human work is also a false choice. In analysing the performance of more than a thousand companies across twelve industries, recent global research has found that firms achieve the most significant performance improvements when humans and machines work together. Companies that most holistically embraced the principles of human–machine collaboration saw more than thrice the level of operational performance improvements as those that used AI tools to substitute for workers. In one example, an American healthcare company saved years of R&D work by having software identify dangerous drug combinations. This left its human researchers with safer avenues to explore.[7]

As the researchers point out: 'What comes naturally to people (making a joke, for example) can be tricky for machines, and what's straightforward for machines (analysing gigabytes of data) remains virtually impossible for humans. Business requires both kinds of capabilities.'[8]

We must see our world as a physical–digital place. A purely 'physical' mindset can make us invest in more physical infrastructure when a digital solution could potentially address our needs more efficiently. In the same way, a purely 'digital' mindset can make us miss physical constraints and goals. It is only when we combine both perspectives in a complementary way that we will make the most out of existing infrastructure, build new infrastructure to be future-ready, and ensure that technology delivers the results we need from it.

One area where the Tata Group has translated this belief into action is in conducting education and employment testing. In the past, for someone living outside a major metro or state capital, the process of giving an entrance exam began with travelling great distances to the nearest testing centre. Candidates had to go where the testers were. The costs of travel and living were the candidates' to bear. All this happened because the task of testing was highly centralized and dependent on the physical presence of testers.

TCS iON, a strategic business unit of TCS, reimagined the process of conducting assessments in a physical–digital manner. Turning a physical-only, centralized and sequential task into one that is managed both physically and digitally, allows it to be distributed and managed in parallel by different resources across the country. As a result, exams today look nothing like they did a decade ago. Physical examination centres, connected to a digital platform, proliferate in small cities and towns. A computer adaptive test adjusts difficulty levels to candidates' performance. Grading, if not automated, is done in a distributed manner by evaluators on the platform. Gaming the system is almost impossible.

Results that took weeks and months previously, are available within a few days, and are more accurate. Access opens up as applicants find assessment centres, previously limited to the big cities, closer home. More than 20,000 jobs have been generated or made more productive, including test centre managers, invigilators and evaluators. The model can scale up to other examinations, evaluators and geographies rapidly. Last year alone, more than 50 million candidates carried out examinations via the physical–digital assessment model, nearly half of whom came from small-town India.

The same can happen in a number of other fields, such as the judiciary, logistics and agriculture.

The third lesson is that we need to grasp the shape and sprawl of technology adoption. The adoption of technology is not only about being able to invent the technology itself; it is also about when the technology becomes affordable enough, and when the social, legal, and political moment is right. Tractors are an example. The potential for farmers all over the world to use tractors has been 100 per cent since at least the 1930s, when they became cost effective. But it was not until 1969 that 80 per cent of farmers in the United States owned tractors. In India, through the 1990s, less than 10 per cent of farms of any size owned a tractor, a mechanized plough or a thresher. The slow adoption of tractors in India was due to their cost and the small size of plots for the most part, but there was also resistance to the new machines from workers and managers.

The spread of automation will take time—it will progress in waves, across different sectors, at different periods, and at different intensities. When it comes to automation in India's economy, certain sectors, especially high-productivity ones that are integrated into global supply chains, might feel its touch earlier, while the rest of the economy may go without seeing substantial change for years. This is true across different sectors, as it is across distinct geographies. This, in itself, is an opportunity. It allows us to design for the future.

How we use this long runway matters a great deal. Since Bridgital is all about marrying people with technology, those employed in Bridgital roles will gain vital skills in working and interacting with new-age technologies. 'Bridgital graduates', armed with these transferable technology skills, can galvanize productivity across sectors. In a future of work transformed by the Fourth Industrial Revolution, where every sector adopts technology to a lesser or greater degree, these skills will allow employees of Bridgital projects to move diagonally to other sectors. This will create the essential ramp we need for people to move from the informal sector to the formal, from unskilled to skilled. As Bridgital graduates go on to join other sectors with higher demand and rewards for their skills, less qualified workers can get on the Bridgital ramp. In this vision, the future of training and skilling will be less about specific industries and roles, and more about digital skills (understanding how to interact with technology), twenty-first-century skills (such as critical thinking, creativity and collaboration), and lifelong learning.

Given the need for a large number of jobs for India's incoming workforce, the country should use the opportunity that technology provides to *generate* gainful employment, instead of investing blindly in labour-substituting automation.

We should also attempt to bridge the increasingly split nature of India's economy, which has a high-productivity formal sector and a low-productivity informal sector, but is missing a middle of intermediate-productivity, mid-skill work. Many workers in the informal sector are trapped in low-wage, low-productivity employment. They struggle to find jobs in which new skills can be learned, skills that can grant them opportunities in the formal sector. Meanwhile, companies struggle to find the skilled workers they need. The repercussions of the 'missing middle' are increasingly visible. India needs a bridge between the two—a bridge by which lower-qualified workers can acquire the digital skills required to participate in the growth story.

This is the opportunity before us, the chance to solve some of our most intractable problems. But it needs our collective intervention, and active participation, to boost jobs and train our workforce for a digital future.

WHAT IS BRIDGITAL?

At its heart, Bridgital addresses access challenges through a reimagining of the tasks and processes that make up a job, and complementing this with technology that enhances and supports workers. Its innovations span three elements.

Bridgital processes

- Redefine what exactly is needed to deliver a service or solution, especially in a manner that prioritizes the challenges of those without access. As this takes place, a lot of activity currently in the purview of the informal sector is brought into the formal fold.

- Rethink conventional approaches to who-does-what in the value-chain of service delivery.

Bridgital technology

- Digital technology and low-cost service delivery models that push the limits of how efficiently we can make use of valuable assets such as physical infrastructure, and the time of high-skill workers.

Bridgital workers

- Digitally literate and technology-augmented workers take on tasks of higher value carved out for them. These range from tasks currently performed by more highly qualified workers, to tasks that mediate likely user challenges in implementing solutions or adopting new services.
- Augmented capabilities of all levels of workers improve the quality, transparency and standardisation of service delivery.

The healthcare system showcases the transformative potential of the Bridgital approach. We cover it in depth in the sections 'The Access Challenge' and 'Bridgital in Action'.

The Access Challenge

4

Calculations

Another phone call. Dulal Pal was fifty years old. A doctor in Tripura recently diagnosed him with jaundice. He wanted to come to Silchar for further consultations right away. Nikhil asked Pal to meet him at the car beside the highway.

At 10 p.m. the next day, Pal and his wife joined the long queue that ended at Nikhil. One psychiatry appointment, one neurology consult, three kidney stones, one stomach problem, and three transportation bookings later, it was Pal's turn to explain what ailed him. The symptoms didn't look like jaundice to Nikhil, but in keeping with his self-imposed rules he didn't offer a diagnosis. Instead, he organized Pal's tests and appointments, and arranged a meeting with a doctor at Cachar Cancer Hospital. Nikhil's brother arrived to drive Pal and his wife to a hut with bamboo walls, reserved for them for ₹120 ($1.70) a night.

The following day, Nikhil took Pal to the diagnostic centre, but the CT scanner wasn't working. A replacement tube was on the way from Guwahati, three hundred kilometres away. The journey would take three days. Nikhil estimated that eight days would pass before all of Pal's reports were ready. Pal was unprepared for this delay. He had shut his shop back home to seek treatment, and was losing money each day he spent in Silchar. Still, he had little choice but to wait.

The diagnosis confirmed Nikhil's hunch. Pal had a tumour in his abdomen. But the patient was just as worried about the money he was losing. Between the shop and his cancer, Pal decided to go home, get the business running again, and then decide what he would do. Weeks later, he called Nikhil. 'So how much money do you think I will need for my treatment? What are the chances of being cured?' he asked. 'How many more years will I live? Does it come back?'

Pal's was one of three cancer diagnoses among patients that arrived for Nikhil from Tripura in the last week of July 2018. All of them returned home after the diagnosis—to balance their budgets, protect their cashflows, weigh potential outcomes, and decide whether to take up the course of treatment their doctors advised. Nikhil knew which way cases like these usually went. Confronted with the prospect of long periods of hospitalization, whose cost was compounded by the days of lost income, patients chose to skip treatment altogether.

Nikhil answered the questions as best he could. He did not expect to hear from Pal again.

●——●

In 2017, an informal survey of patients living on the streets outside Tata Memorial Hospital found that they had lost an average of ₹55,000 ($786) in foregone wages during the course of their treatment. Nearly half of the patients had worked as daily-wage labourers. When they returned home, there was no guarantee they would find such work again.[1]

So many Indians live on the edge of poverty that it only takes one adverse health event to tip them over. Every year, as many as 49 million Indians are pushed into poverty by medical expenses—over half of the 97 million people around the world who fall into poverty when a catastrophic health event occurs.[2] The cost of healthcare can lead to a spiral of debt. Their standard of living falls, opportunities vanish, and a vicious cycle that may span generations sets in. The full cost to India, especially in terms of the incredible potential that goes undeveloped and unrealized as a result, can only be described as a national tragedy.

5

The Great Medical Migration

Set against India's rapid economic growth, its healthcare record is bleak. In 2016, the country's communicable diseases death rate was starkly higher than the global average. There are more tuberculosis patients per 100,000 people than in Uganda, Afghanistan and Haiti. India has much higher maternal and infant mortality rates than countries in the region such as Mongolia, Sri Lanka and Vietnam.[1]

Much of this is because India's public health system is understaffed and underfunded. This is especially the case in rural India's network of primary and community health centres.[2] The lack of reliable access to doctors and medicines at rural public health facilities leaves patients seeking care from sources they trust, such as family, elders and local healers, rather than trained doctors. And when trusted sources fail, patients travel, often great distances—not just to the large, super-speciality hospitals in the big metros, but to public hospitals in every state capital, and even tertiary hospitals in district capitals. This is the great medical migration: Millions of people travelling great distances to large urban hospitals that end up bearing the load of primary and secondary health centres.

Tata Memorial Centre in Mumbai mapped the location of 75,000 patients and found that over half travelled more than a thousand kilometres to get access to reliable cancer treatment. Granted, patients the world over may have to travel to access specialized care for cancer. Innovative models have emerged in response to these challenges, such as the distributed cancer control model pioneered by Tata Trusts.[3] In India today, however, many are travelling with more routine complaints. Delhi's All India Institute of Medical Sciences sees 9,000 patients at its outpatient clinics every day. Some may have nothing more serious than a viral infection or fever, which could easily be addressed at a primary care clinic. The large numbers are not easily served. They stretch India's hospitals—already brimming with patients and renowned for their efficiency—to breaking point, and force them into innovation of a different kind. 'We admit a patient here only if she agrees to share her bed with another patient,' a staff member at the Government Medical College in Dehradun says. 'We don't have enough beds, but they keep pouring in.'[4]

In the mind of patients exposed to India's medical system, there is either the most basic healthcare, or large hospitals. Between these, there is nowhere else to go.

6

Twice Exceptional

Between 2018 and 2019, we and our team of researchers travelled frequently to India's north-east, which has among the highest cancer rates in the country (largely linked to the widespread use of tobacco). We focused on Barak Valley in Assam to understand how hospitals were coping with a constant flood of patients.[1]

The valley is twice an exception: It is in a region struck by exceptional rates of cancer, and is also shaped by exceptional and dedicated healthcare providers. Nowhere is this more apparent than in the city of Silchar, a place overrun with patients and a commercial ecosystem that serves all their needs. There are pharmacies at every corner. Off the busy Meherpur Road, a string of hospitals cater to the rich and the poor. A billboard for a healthcare brand features an illustration of a pawn toppling the king on a chessboard. 'One right decision can conquer cancer,' it reads.

Cancer makes healthcare more complex, and also exposes its limits. The illness demands consistent engagement with a higher level of expertise, found mostly in the formal health system. This means that patients have to overcome social, physical, financial and geographic hurdles before they meet a doctor who can help. The constraints are multilayered, and often prohibitively high.

How patients and medical staff in the north-east cope with cancer provides some insight into India's larger healthcare challenges.

•——•

We first visited Kalyani Hospital, which resembled, on the outside, an ordinary two-storey building. It was late in the afternoon, and the sky was quickly turning dark. There were hundreds of tired patients thronging the halls on every floor. We went up to the second floor to meet Dr Das, who had asked Nikhil to transport the hospital's patients years ago. Upstairs, we waited in a consultation room with desks and plastic chairs while his secretary explained that he was performing a surgery. We had arrived on a day booked for operations. Dr Das and his staff assembled in the operating theatre before 9 a.m., and ended work twelve hours later. Each doctor performed up to ten operations a day. This was why the staff looked exhausted, his secretary explained apologetically.

Dr Das arrived in his operating coat, jeans, and a cap. A native of Silchar, Dr Das could speak at great length about airflow control in operating theatres, post-operative wound dressings, and the preventive use of antibiotics. Some of his ideas put him at odds with accepted practice of larger hospitals, but also put him on the same plane as his patients, whose needs and constraints he put above almost every other concern.

'Giving a prescription is very easy,' he said. 'But when our patients do not have even one square meal a day, how can they follow the course of medicine post-treatment?' He said the hospital treated nearly fifteen thousand patients on a budget of about two and a half crore rupees every year ($350,000, or less than $1,000 per day)—a remarkably small sum. There was no place for excess of any kind. He led us to a room where the beds were set right beside each other. Nurses squeezed between them to reach patients. 'People say that you shouldn't have a cramped room, and that there should be more space,' Dr Das said. 'But it actually helps us because one nurse can see and can take care of so many more patients at the same time.'

Now the director and head surgeon at Kalyani Hospital, Dr Das joined its staff over three decades ago, in 1987. He left a successful private practice in the United States, turned away from the lucrative opportunities available in India's big city hospitals, and followed his heart to his hometown, the 'green and Bengali-speaking' Silchar, he said. Decades here had made him a veteran of medical life on the frontline, where an absence of resources made the simplest procedures challenging. His patients travelled hundreds of kilometres for basic surgeries: Gall bladder stones, kidney stones, an appendectomy.

There was no respite. Even after hours, when the outpatient department was closed and he was at home, sipping on lemon tea and reading the day's news, patients approached him for an after-hours consultation. He was seventy-seven, and had deep reserves of energy. His tireless service earned him a nickname from locals: They called him *bhagwan*, God.

As we spoke, he guided us to a room next door. People lay on operating tables. The room was the size of a handful of cubicles, and contained three beds with three patients undergoing surgery that moment. Doctors' elbows touched as they made incisions on different patients. One nurse bumped into another while she changed an intravenous line. Dr Das didn't have enough time to sit and talk, so he kept chatting while he performed a lumpectomy.

Dr Das was proud of the operation theatre staff he had trained. They were efficient, and made do with very little. But recruiting and retaining a quality medical team was a problem, he said. There were staff shortages every day. The choice, for many of them, was between a comfortable life and a fulfilling one. Twelve of the hospital's sixteen doctors were over sixty. Young doctors tended to have other priorities.

Many of the support staff did not have a degree. Only three nurses had formal degrees in general nursing and midwifery. Physicians did not have assistants. The head administrator's position was honorary, and currently occupied by a retired bank official. Dr Das seemed to spend as much time on paperwork and raising funds as he did on surgeries. To a visitor, many of his daily duties were not among a senior surgeon's core responsibilities. He, and the other staff, needed to be everywhere because there simply weren't enough people.

Every day, the younger staff offered advice on how Kalyani could upgrade its operations. Dr Das found the suggestions unhelpful. 'Any improvement that makes this hospital feel inaccessible to the poor defeats our purpose,' he told them. Before our visit, he was deciding whether to purchase an oxygen machine or a CT scanner. The hospital needed both, but could only afford one or the other.

Corporate hospitals and private nursing homes tended to have the best equipment and facilities; the government-run medical colleges provided free or highly subsidized care, but very few were able to maintain consistently high standards. A hospital like Kalyani bridged the two ends: Better care at prices dictated by the patients' ability to pay.

On the wall of the main outpatient department, the hospital displayed a rate chart with fees that were at least half those charged in other facilities. The rates had been revised in 2015, but none of that mattered to patients. Prices old or new, everything was only the start of a long negotiation that usually ended in free treatment. Dr Das estimated that almost half of his patients couldn't afford the official rate, and about five per cent paid nothing at all. That was why, even though Tripura had government medical colleges, its people crossed state borders to seek treatment in Silchar. They knew that good doctors and a benevolent hospital awaited them.

All of this came at a cost patients did not see: The hospital was running at a loss.

Everything required money. There was never enough money. Yes, there were philanthropic gestures, but there was no telling what form donations could take. One time, a large oil exploration company decided it would be socially responsible by donating a thousand metal pipes to Kalyani hospital, which happened to be close to its facility in Assam, rather than shipping the pipes hundreds of kilometres to the nearest large city for auction. For months, the thousand metal pipes lay behind the hospital while Dr Das wondered what to do with the generous donation. One day, perhaps out of desperation, or out of exasperation, or even out of his instinct to stretch every possible resource, Dr Das used them as a barrier against landslides, and to shield plastic water pipes from the monkeys who swung on them.

Dr Das and the hospital's ageing committee members worried about the future. They were enterprising, and relied on *jugaad*—temporary measures widely celebrated as Indian resourcefulness—more often than they liked, but knew that philanthropy and scavenging could not keep the hospital running. It was unsustainable.

'I imagine Kalyani will become like any other nursing home or hospital—more mercenary than missionary,' Dr Das said. 'We'll have to charge a lot to the patients, earn a lot, and spend a lot on doctors.' The thought upset him. 'I would hate to see our mission change, even if we really are running in the red. Our aim is and always has been to give cheap but good care to those who need it.'

He threw up his hands. 'To do anything less would be a sad fate for a place like this. What would happen to our patients?'

7

The Big Disease

Cachar Cancer Hospital was on the north-western edge of Silchar, about 10 kilometres away from Kalyani Hospital, but the journey was slow and halting. Signs of prosperity and progress stood along the road: Innumerable building sites, trucks carrying construction material, and traffic squeezing into every gap to be found.

Inside the cancer hospital, the head physician flipped through a patient's medical file. With salt-and-pepper hair cropped short and razor-straight posture, he had the air of a military general. His manner with patients, though, was gentle and calming. He was speaking with an elderly lady, who had been advised to undergo surgery, but was frightened by the prospect of an operation. He spoke softly. 'This is a big decision, and it is important that you take the time to think it over. Go home, take some rest, and you will do what's right.'

As he stepped outside, patients swarmed around him immediately. Walking the length of the hall took at least twenty minutes. Two members of the hospital staff chased after him, waving an equipment purchase form that needed multiple signatures, and also to let him know about a package for delivery. A number of patients made emotional appeals to him to personally perform their surgeries. A woman, nearly bald from chemotherapy, said, 'Will my son also get cancer? Everyone tells me he will. He is only ten years old.'

'No, he won't,' the doctor said patiently, amid the chaos. 'There's no truth to that. Cancer can happen to anyone, but just because you have cancer doesn't mean he will too.'

'Oh, thank you. Even if he doesn't eat properly? He refuses to eat meat. Will he be okay?'

The doctor laughed. 'Neither do I! He will be just fine.'

On the other side of the hospital, three young women waited anxiously near the outpatient department. They were dressed in Khasi attire: a bright blouse and skirt, a chequered shawl knotted at the shoulder and draped across their bodies. They formed a protective circle around Lariti Nongrum's four-year-old son Headingson, trying to shield him from the light drizzle. Nestled in a sheet slung across her back, Headingson burrowed closer to his mother. Lariti named him Headingson because he was her firstborn. She imagined that he would one day head a tribe of his brothers and sisters.

The Big Disease

They had travelled over three hours and some 70 kilometres from their village, Byndihati, in Meghalaya. The village was remote. There was no power, and water was difficult to find. When it rained, Lariti left open plastic containers outside. The family of five ate whatever grew on the trees nearby. The previous year, they had earned no more than ₹60,000 ($860) by selling the harvest from the betel nut trees outside their home.

A month before their visit, Headingson was walking home from school when he stumbled and fell. By the time he reached home, his upper right leg was painfully swollen, but there was no visible cut or scrape on his skin. His family applied herbal oils to the afflicted area, to ease the swelling and make the pain go away.

A week ago, Headingson could manage a shaky walk. Now, he groaned every time his foot touched the ground. Headingson could not bear the pain any more. His leg was disfigured. Lariti decided it was time for more definitive medical action.

A nurse saw the X-ray of Headingson's leg and scheduled an appointment with a surgical oncologist. For two hours they waited silently outside his room. Then the oncologist called them in, assessed Headingson's thigh, and told them it was a tumour. He ordered an MRI and tests to assess the size and progress of the tumour. This was vital. It was possible to cure bone tumours that had not spread if the conditions were favourable.

In shock, the family turned to leave as quickly as possible. They paid for the consultation without a word.

The family discussed their doubts about the diagnosis. They did not trust the doctor. How could someone so tiny have 'the big disease'? Was the hospital just trying to make money off their fears? To compound matters, they had already spent a meaningful portion of their annual earnings on this trip. They decided to head home and get another opinion later, preferably at a hospital in Shillong with Khasi staff.

Their mistake became all too clear when Headingson's illness worsened back home. Only then, all too late, the family decided that he would undergo proper treatment at any cost. Once more they undertook the long journey to Shillong, and did tests that cost them a full year's income. The new tests showed them that the wait had proved fatal. The cancer had spread. A Khasi doctor asked Lariti why they hadn't come sooner. But to Lariti, the doctors and hospitals had been alien, and she hadn't believed them when they said that Headingson had cancer.

One day, six months after Headingson had died, Lariti finally stepped out of her home. She walked down an uneven path carefully, between the betel trees, until she came to the river near their house, one that separated India and Bangladesh. The water gurgled as it rushed past her, birds cried around her, and the household's voices were behind her, but the sound she heard most clearly was silence.

8

Out of Reach

How did India get here? How did it end up with a patchwork healthcare system where patients believe that opting out of life-saving treatment is in their best interest?

We believe this is a story about good intentions that went awry, at whose heart lies a brutally simple explanation: An endemic shortage of medical personnel.

In 1946, the Health Survey and Development Committee made a crucial decision to give Indians access to high-quality healthcare by turning the district public health system into a three-tier model (primary, secondary and district-level), with each level staffed by trained medical officers.[1]

The Committee, also known as the Bhore Committee, was set up in 1943 to devise a single national standard for the healthcare sector—a necessity, since healthcare in pre-Independence India was fragmented and uneven, regulated by provincial governments, each in their own areas. At the time, there were about 47,000 registered practitioners of allopathic medicine. A little over a third of them were university graduates, who had been through a five-and-a-half-year course in a medical college—the equivalent of a graduate doctor today. Two-thirds were licentiates—lesser qualified practitioners who went through shorter three- or four-year courses in medical schools. It was these licentiates who, besides practitioners of traditional systems of medicine, delivered much of rural healthcare.[2]

The Committee was concerned about the quality and completeness of training licentiates had received, and of their ability to deliver effective care. 'Having regard to the limited resources available for the training of doctors,' it recommended that the country direct all efforts to the production of 'basic doctors', with the minimum acceptable training of five-and-a-half years.[3] Only these most highly qualified doctors would be allowed to treat patients. In one swoop, they set aside the entire range of licentiates and indigenous 'semi-doctors', who were the only kind of health providers close enough and inexpensive enough to meet the needs and means of most Indians.

This meant that while India was given excellent medical standards, there were never enough doctors to practise those standards.

Fast forward to today. Official figures based on the set of doctors registered with the Medical Council of India (MCI) show India having just over a million doctors. This means there are about 8 doctors for every 10,000 residents, a ratio similar to that in South Africa, Vietnam and Thailand.[4] The MCI's registry, however, includes doctors registered to practise in India since 1961. A more realistic ratio would be closer to 5 doctors per 10,000 population, estimated from a 2017 study in the *Indian Journal of Public Health* that adjusted the registry figures to account for doctors who had emigrated, left the profession or died. In contrast, China has a doctor-to-population ratio three times this adjusted figure.[5]

These are all indicators, but the disparity they reflect is real. It will take approximately 600,000 more doctors and nearly 2.5 million more nurses for India to reach the minimum population coverage levels recommended by the World Health Organisation. This means nearly doubling the number of its current practising doctors if the country hopes to provide a basic level of care.[6]

At the level of specializations, the pinch is even more acute. A 2014 study in *The Lancet* found that India had approximately 2,000 surgical oncologists and radiologists. India needs double that number, if not more, given the number of new cancer cases emerging every year. The situation looks even worse in fields that have typically received less attention, such as mental health, where there may be only a few trained professionals for millions of citizens.[7]

What's worse: Almost 65 per cent of the country's medical practitioners—doctors, dentists, physiotherapists, nurses, health assistants and registered practitioners of traditional systems—are based in urban India.[8] Meanwhile, about 67 per cent of the country lives in areas considered rural. If you're in Delhi or Mumbai, there's no shortage of doctors. If you're outside the big towns and cities, finding solid medical advice is an ordeal.

This chasm between where authorized medical practitioners are, and where patients live, is at the heart of the access predicament in Indian healthcare. The fact is that India's healthcare system demands a great migration from those it would heal, across geographies, across financial compulsions, across language barriers, and across deep-rooted belief systems—a migration that few have the resources to undertake.

9

Imbalances

It has been clear for some time to those who use India's healthcare system: It does not work. Primary health centres and sub-centres are at the frontlines of the public health system, and they exist in a constant state of shortage and disrepair. In theory, each primary health centre is supposed to serve a population of 25,000. In practice, though, some of the nearly 26,000 centres serve triple that number.[1]

Across the country, nearly one in three primary health centres lacks a labour room. A similar number have fewer than the four hospital beds mandated for each centre. Only a fifth of all primary health centres have two doctors, the very minimum required number. Many states report shortfalls in required medication and, in one survey, almost half of all doctors and healthcare staff were missing from their posts on any given day.[2]

With nowhere to turn, and unsure of doctors at primary health centres, patients seek out their own solutions to problems. They ask for a second opinion in their community, or turn to a local traditional healer for help.

They are entirely rational in doing so.

In 2014, for a study led by researchers at the World Bank, actors were trained to visit healthcare facilities and complain about symptoms that corresponded with common illnesses that people in the area suffered from.[3] The actors were dispatched to public health centres (with a formally qualified doctor), private clinics run by unqualified practitioners, and private clinics run by qualified doctors. The fake patients were trained to assess the quality of care they received on various parameters, including the time each doctor spent with them, whether the doctor asked them relevant questions, the provision and accuracy of the diagnosis (given the symptoms the 'patients' reported), and whether the treatment prescribed was correct.

The study found that there was no difference in the quality of care between a government-run public health centre and an unqualified doctor. The quality of care only improved if patients met qualified doctors outside public health centres, such as at their private practice. Even then, patients felt better cared for by unqualified doctors, who asked them more questions, than by qualified public-sector doctors, who tended to rush through the consultation. This may explain why unqualified medical practitioners account for the larger share of rural primary care visits.[4]

Over time, the experiences of patients and communities have hardened into expectation. It is taken for granted that doctors, medicines, time, and even physical clinics are scarce. Even when they are available, they will be of limited benefit. Patients who can afford private treatment bypass the public system altogether, creating a feedback loop where doctors and health workers are drawn into the private system as well. Others who cannot find a private health provider in their own area, travel to the largest, most reputable public hospitals. And some find healthcare so expensive, they endure illness instead of seeking treatment.

As a result, while the primary healthcare network is underutilized and widely distrusted, the secondary and tertiary hospitals are swamped with far more patients than they were ever designed to serve. A well-intentioned system, designed to provide the highest quality of care to the largest number of people, has instead driven them away. They can pay to see private care providers, or crowd into the halls of increasingly overburdened public hospitals. The tertiary care hospitals—meant to be centres of emergency and specialized care—are struggling under a burden of cases that should have been resolved elsewhere.

The cost of this topsy-turvy world is very real. Because healthcare isn't close to where they live, patients travel great distances, to new and unfamiliar places, to seek advice. There, language and culture gets in the way. They mistrust specialists, and turn to informal practitioners who speak their language. While they may receive good care in certain environments, the risks stemming from oversight run high.

One such case in early 2018 involved an unlicensed, self-styled doctor in the Unnao district of Uttar Pradesh, who may have infected dozens of his patients with HIV when he reused infected needles. Chief among his virtues for his patients was that he visited their neighbourhood on his bicycle, and charged only ₹10 ($0.15) to treat them.[5]

The service was a fraud, but the need is genuine.

The irony of India's healthcare sector is that this patchwork domestic healthcare system sits alongside a flourishing medical tourism sector which treats roughly 500,000 foreign patients a year and is set to grow to $7–8 billion by 2020.[6] India clearly has the potential to deliver the highest standards of medical care; the challenge is in turning this potential into reliable and affordable access for the majority of Indians who cannot afford to seek care at high-end private hospitals.

Timing is important. A working primary health system isn't just necessary to handle the pressures of today, but the problems of tomorrow. India is going through an epidemiological transition. It is confronted by an increasing prevalence of non-communicable diseases that are now the largest contributor to illness and death in India, in addition to infectious and nutritional diseases common in many low- and lower-middle income countries. Non-communicable diseases like diabetes and heart ailments are typically chronic, requiring periodic visits to a health facility. Beyond genetic factors, they are largely tied to lifestyle choices.[7]

Primary care providers play a pivotal role in prevention education and early detection, and primary care is the key way to treat chronic diseases at scale. To do so, the system needs to be made more available, accessible and functional.

10

Outreach

A more effective public health system is in everyone's interests, but effectiveness requires large-scale interventions. Recently, to help stem the cost of healthcare for its poorest, India introduced the National Health Protection Scheme, the world's largest healthcare scheme. 'Ayushman Bharat Yojana', as the programme is formally called, will provide about 500 million low-income Indians with free health cover for a range of treatments that require hospitalization.[1] This should place life-saving care in the reach of households that could not have afforded it before.

Ayushman Bharat will go a long way in relieving pressure on Indians, but for the programme to be truly effective, it needs to succeed in quickly improving primary care—a stated but less discussed aim. Without fortifying this layer of the health system, insurance will only send more people to the already stressed secondary and tertiary tier of healthcare.

Increasing public financing, putting better procurement procedures in place, and providing more insurance options can all help improve healthcare. But it isn't enough. Healthcare can't be tinkered with any more; it needs to be transformed. Education needs to be stepped up; regulation needs to be made more flexible. The healthcare sector needs to use existing resources more efficiently, and explore the potential of digitally-enabled systems to create new resources.

Roles need to be reimagined. Instead of relying predominantly on doctors, a separate cadre of health administrators could take on administrative tasks. Electronic medical records could be made available any time and any where to patients and their doctors—whether today, ten years later, or half a century later. A new force of lower-qualified workers (such as health assistants, especially for rural India) could build on the success of India's community health worker model and deliver essential services cheaply in the most distant reaches of the country.

At the same time, a large swathe of currently informal roles, like Nikhil's, can be brought into the formal fold: Their contribution acknowledged and documented with real-time record keeping; their capacity enhanced by establishing proper protocols and providing training; and their own income and job security improved by affiliation with a formal institution.

To do this, India's health system must be fixed from the bottom up, and this must happen with the workers and resources it already has. What's common to all the solutions mentioned above is innovative, advanced technology. The country simply cannot afford to wait for new doctors to turn up and fill its vacancies.

11

Bridging Access

If the healthcare needs of Indians, especially in rural India, are to be addressed reliably and effectively, trust and community are vital. This means healthcare close to home. That is where hurdles to access should be removed.

It is at the primary health centre itself that patients and providers are most familiar and comfortable with one another. They speak the same language, their concerns overlap.

With improvements in primary care, expenses will decline. Patients will no longer need to travel long distances and sacrifice earnings.

The benefits will trickle up.

If larger hospitals are not inundated with more patients than they can manage, the quality of service they can offer—as well as the experience of working in a hospital itself—will see dramatic improvements.

All these transformations will only happen with a new approach to healthcare. A health sector rife with scarcity at every level of expertise will not be able to see more patients and provide better care. It will not be able to address the access challenge to any significant degree, any time soon. India doesn't just need more doctors, it needs a better-designed healthcare system that makes smarter use of clinically trained personnel.

Healthcare is just one of the innumerable areas where the access challenge rears its head. But it is an essential example to understand. It spans the many dimensions of struggle that translate into bleak statistics. The lack of skilled workers. The problems with quality. The breakdown of systems. The inordinate burdens placed on patients, and how their responses reinforce the status quo. The sheer frustration— on the part of both patient and provider—of living through the systemic deficits of access.

India's access challenge has many faces and affects hundreds of millions. These themes play out in variations of degree and form across different sectors.

Education. The gap in the number of teachers is large, though not as problematic as that of doctors and nurses. Quality and consistency are the defining issues. So, too, are the pressures on their time, limiting their ability to train themselves, dedicate time for lesson planning, and provide students individual attention. Students suffer the consequences. India's poor education outcomes are well-documented. Enrolment drops off from around 97 per cent in elementary school to about 56 per cent in higher secondary school, and 25 per cent at university level. In rural India, a little over half the children enrolled in fifth grade can read a second-grade text, and less than 30 per cent in the third grade are able to do basic arithmetic like subtraction. The gap in grade-appropriate skills persists through school and college, and as they make their way into the workforce.[1]

Logistics. Being a truck driver in India means long hours and distances traversed, with little by way of returns. Finding work can be a regular struggle, followed by weeks on end away from home, and a gruelling quality of life on the road. It is no wonder India has a reported 22 per cent shortage in commercial vehicle drivers.[2] It is typical, but misguided, to blame drivers for the delays, transit losses and goods damage that result in the high cost of moving goods in India. A systemic fix is needed. Micro, and small and medium businesses feel the logistics access gap the most. Farmers feel it as well, along with the larger agriculture networks located outside urban and peri-urban transport hubs.

Judiciary. The judicial system is no different from most other sectors when it comes to shortfalls of manpower and efficiency. There are more than 30 million cases pending before the different levels of India's judiciary, while nearly a quarter of sanctioned judicial posts lie vacant. A time-use study of district courts in one of India's states shows that as much as 30–50 per cent of judges' time may be devoted to hearings that are primarily administrative or procedural in nature. Unsurprisingly, delays and deferments are rife. Delays in criminal matters disproportionately affect the poor, who are unable to afford bail. Delays in civil and commercial matters give rise to India's rank of 163 out of 190 countries on the 'enforcing contracts and efficiency of judicial system' metric of the World Bank's latest ease of doing business survey.[3]

•—•

Part of the answer to the access challenge is making better use of the facilities India already has, in ways hitherto unexplored. Digital approaches can reimagine service delivery, and decentralized technologies can shorten the distance between people and systems. This is what Bridgital seeks to address.

The other part is about making better use of the human capital available to India. It demands a more thoughtful approach to our people and our potential. It is about designing diverse channels for people of different education and skills levels to move flexibly and match job opportunities. Here too, people need lower barriers to access. As the next chapter will show, the challenges that affect India don't require a miracle to solve. The resources needed are abundant. They only need a conducive setting to flourish.

XX Factor—The Talent Dividend

12

An Unlikely Officer

Whenever Bathinda's marital problems got out of hand, they became Jasleen Kaur's problems.[1] Every morning, the women's cell officer arrived at the police station and sat on the same swivel chair, the light from outside falling on her large wooden desk, in a room with iron and wood cabinets full of cases from all over town. They never stopped coming.

Among the files placed on her desk for her immediate attention was one such case—a woman whose businessman husband had tortured her for durable goods and furniture, and then tortured her some more for a car. The stories melted into each other. The Bathinda women's cell that she was a part of had become involved in so many disputes that the godown they ran had no more room to store disputed dowry gifts.[2] Jasleen had come to believe that all this could be avoided if women were more educated.

In her early thirties, Jasleen was filled with notions of justice, but she knew that, sometimes, hashing out differences was better than the grind of the law. Nobody wanted that. She preferred to resolve cases outside the system, before they became cases, by taking everyone aside to have a quiet chat. This involved persuading husbands and in-laws to behave themselves and receive mandatory counselling. If the approach worked, wives returned home.

At other times, the patterns of behaviour Jasleen was called on to stop were simply too far gone, and she advised victims to pack up their things and leave. These were the extreme cases, where in-laws questioned a woman's character and integrity, and the abuse was so intense that Jasleen had to step in to counsel the woman. Those cases went to court, requiring her to deal with gathering mountains of evidence, and shepherding everyone into court for hearings. The paperwork was a bother, and court took up a lot of time, but it was all preferable to dealing with dowry deaths. Those she really struggled with.

When they spoke about her, her colleagues could see only her calmness and composure. They praised her track record, which they all thought commendable. The sub-inspector had official admiration for her: 'Jasleen not only tries to solve these cases without pushing the family into any legal problem, but also ensures that the victim is not harassed until a decision is taken on the matter.' In turn, Jasleen was grateful for the support they gave her.

Technically speaking, Jasleen was an outlier, and that she had come far enough to a high-ranking position at the women's cell at Bathinda was a matter of quiet pride. But the seeds of her success were sown before she was born, of this she was sure. Her father, a rural daily-wage worker, and her mother, Amanjot Kaur, were both convinced that their children had to receive an education. As a Dalit family, they had witnessed first-hand the caste discrimination that hobbles generations. Amanjot remembered days when there was little to eat because her husband's earnings were spent on the children's studies. 'Being a Dalit with four children and no financial resources was a burden on my life,' she said. Life only improved once her elder sons began to work.

When the 2011 census data was published, it showed that Giana, the village where Jasleen was born, had a literacy rate of about 57 per cent, well below the overall state literacy rate of 76 per cent. The literacy rate for women in Giana was even worse, because women simply did not complete their education.

It was clear, very early on, that Jasleen would chart a different path. Jasleen, her mother recalled, had a relentless curiosity beyond her textbooks. Her friends remembered her as one of the few students devoted to school. The government schools she attended were near the village, and they welcomed students of every caste. It was here that she began to dream of becoming a teacher.

In 2007, her father died. Immediately, Amanjot came under pressure to have Jasleen married. Jasleen wanted no part of it, but she also had very little say in the matter. Amanjot agreed to a proposal from a debt collection agent with a financial services firm, whose father was a retired driver from Punjab's irrigation department. The marriage took place in 2008 in a gurudwara, with close family and friends in attendance. Jasleen was twenty-three. Weddings in Punjab are typically spectacular occasions, but this one was low-key. The families' finances did not allow the slightest extravagance.

13

The Talent Dividend

A ten percentage point increase in India's overall female labour participation 'would surely be the easiest half-trillion-dollar boost available to the global economy.'

—The Economist (July 2018)[1]

In India, a woman's path from education to work is often permanently interrupted—by marriage, family wishes, children, societal pressures. Their absence comes at a cost. India has an enormous number of secondary-educated women who are inaccessible to the workforce.

This means the economy gets hit twice: first, just 33 per cent of all workers in India have a secondary (or above) education.[2] Second, millions of educated people remain outside of the workforce. Nearly 120 million women in India—more than double the entire population of South

Korea—have at least a secondary education, but do not participate in the workforce.

For a country that needs millions of professionals urgently for vital skilled jobs, these millions of women provide a powerful answer. If even half of this group entered the workforce, the share of workers with at least a secondary education would jump from 33 per cent of the total workforce to 46 per cent—the equivalent of the last decade and a half's worth of improvement in this metric. In one stroke, their engagement could add ₹31 trillion ($440 billion) to India's GDP.[3]

Indian women want to work. Three-quarters of teenage girls in a national survey of over 70,000 girls said they wanted a career after graduating, and expressed specific career aspirations. In a national survey in 2012, when researchers surveyed women engaged in domestic duties, almost one in three said they would accept paid work if a good opportunity arose. If every woman who said they would take up paid work ended up doing so, India's workforce participation for women could touch nearly 80 per cent.[4]

Despite the pressing case for women working, just 23 per cent of Indian working-age women are in the labour force. Among G20 states, India is second-to-last in terms of women's participation, with Saudi Arabia alone ranking lower. India is not only well below its neighbours (roughly 80 per cent of Nepali women work), but also countries of similar income levels.[5]

Women's Labour Force Participation Noticeably Lags in India

Women's Labour Force Participation Rate by Country/Region

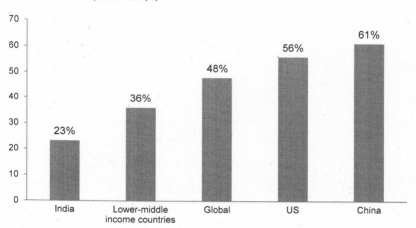

Labour Force Participation Rate (%)

Source: India—Periodic Labour Force Survey (2017–18); Other countries—ILOSTAT (2018)

Worryingly, trends show that women's work participation in India is not only low, it's falling. At a time when India's economy reportedly grew over 7 per cent on average over the past decade, increased opportunities should have set the stage for a rise in women's work. Instead, the opposite has happened: 19 million fewer women participated in paid work in 2017 than in 2011.

There are complex reasons for the steep decline. Some of them are good. As households have become wealthier, more women have been able to stay in school (this explains a third of the decline). Other trends are more disturbing. In agriculture, a large number of roles that have been mechanized since 2005 belonged to women. Of the jobs created by mechanization, 80 per cent were filled by men. In looking at all the jobs lost across the economy in 2018, the Centre for Monitoring Indian Economy posits that over three-quarters of the jobs lost were held by women.[6]

Talent is universal, but opportunities are not. Correcting this can lend a tremendous boost to growth. We have seen this take place in a global context. *The Economist* expressed the importance of women's work participation best, back in 2006: '. . . the employment of extra women . . . has chipped in [to global GDP growth] more than either capital investment or increased productivity . . . Over the past decade or so, the increased employment of women in developed economies has contributed much more to global growth than China has.' Just imagine: If all of India's states resembled the country's best performer—Karnataka—in terms of female to male ratios in managerial positions, India's economy over the 1961–91 period would have been higher by more than a third.[7]

The case for more women in the workforce is resounding, and India in particular has scope for a large boost to the economy from strategies that raise women's participation in paid work. The last decade of experience and research has brought this opportunity to light. We now need to shift gears and understand better how to make paid work a worthwhile option for women. There are no simple solutions. Bringing about effective change will require India to navigate a complicated web of poorly understood barriers. But it can and must be done, if India is to effectively deal with the immense jobs challenge that is already at its doorstep.

14

The Spark

After they were married, Jasleen made it clear to her husband, Manbir, that she wasn't about to do what everyone before her had done. She wanted to work. He told her that he wanted her to achieve her dreams.

Luck was on Jasleen's side. After the wedding, her father-in-law, Hardeep Singh, asked her if she wanted to continue studying. She told him that she did, and wanted to be a teacher. Hardeep dug deep for his daughter-in-law. The ₹9,500 ($136) pension he received every month made up the bulk of the family's earnings, and never seemed enough to manage its expenses. Somehow, he stretched it just enough to help Jasleen graduate with a degree of Bachelor of Education (BEd) from Punjab University. When Jasleen was studying, villagers came by with unsolicited advice for the family: You shouldn't let your *noo*, your daughter-in-law, get an education.

But Hardeep said what her friends said, what almost anyone who has met Jasleen, says: 'I knew she had a spark.'

After completing her BEd, she tried to qualify as a teacher, but was shattered when she failed the Teacher Eligibility Test by two marks. It was Manbir, then, who asked her what she thought of joining the police. 'My husband was a major support and kept counselling me,' Jasleen said. 'He said that since I could not clear the examination, I could work hard to become a police officer. He had always thought of me joining the police.'

There were other things on Manbir's mind. Poverty and the caste system prevented people from moving above the lowest rung of society. With money and status, those shackles could be broken. 'If you are rich, or have power in your hand, everyone will come to you and your caste will not matter.' Being in the police offered this possibility.

It seemed an impossible dream. When vacancies for the post of sub-inspector in the Punjab Police opened up, Jasleen wondered if she was right for the job.

Her son, Vikram, was only four months old when she filled the form. She left his care to the family, and began working on improving her physical strength, which would be tested during a physical endurance examination. For this, she joined a private academy that trained police and army aspirants, with a focus on both physical training and building mental endurance. 'By filling the form, I had stepped into a new arena and I wanted to carve my future all by myself and not depend on my family. It was this decision that made me stronger.'

When Vikram cried for food, Jasleen would feed him on the training grounds. The other women there didn't understand why her husband and child had to visit. Most of them were single, and in their early twenties. Jasleen was in her late twenties, and subjected to frequent asides that a woman with young children could not become a police officer. She shrugged it off and kept training.

In 2014, Jasleen passed her physical test and her written test, and readied herself for the final hurdle, an interview. She fretted about the repercussions of failure. 'I knew that this was probably my first and last chance. I kept remembering how much trust my family, especially my father-in-law and husband, had in me.'

The interview took place at the state capital, Chandigarh. The interviewers asked Jasleen how she planned to make sure that justice was delivered to the victims whose cases she would handle. It was a question whose answer she had carried within her all her life. She had seen tough days, she told them, and could empathize with others who faced injustice. She would ensure that no one was left disgruntled. They offered her the job. Her village went crazy.

'It was like Diwali.'

15

Twice-Hit Economy

'More girls are being educated than boys. You have to ask, "Where are they going and what are they doing?"'

—Dr Pronab Sen, Country Director, International Growth Centre's (IGC) India Central Programme

In looking at different aspects of women's participation in the labour force, two trends stand out: the pattern of women's participation by education and by age.

At every level of education, one thing is clear: Women have dramatically lower participation rates than men. More curiously, the shape of the participation curve by education resembles a 'U'. Women with very low and very high levels of education tend to participate more than other women in the workforce. There's a missing middle of women with intermediate levels of education, who do not have a presence in the workforce.[1] For women, having more than a basic education doesn't necessarily translate to a boost in their participation in paid work. It could, surprisingly, even lead to a dip.

This is, in part, thanks to something known as the income effect. As households start to become marginally richer, the pressure to do paid work eases and attention turns to domestic duties. More often than not, women end up becoming secondary earners and primary carers. Still, the income effect is only a partial explanation. Indian women's labour participation rates are markedly lower than other countries at similar levels of incomes.

The U-Curve: India's Workforce Is Missing Out on Its Educated Women

Labour Force Participation Rate by Education Level

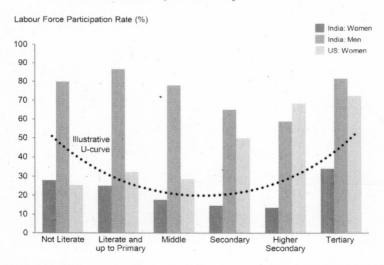

Note: Primary (Class 1–5); Middle (Class 6–8); Secondary (Class 9–10); Higher Secondary (Class 11–12); and Tertiary (post–formal schooling). The categorization for the US may vary slightly as ILOSTAT uses the International Standard of Classification of Education 2011 (ISCED-11) system of educational classification. For comparability, the US data has been approximated closely to India's education categories as provided in the Periodic Labour Force Survey, 2017–18.

Source: India—Periodic Labour Force Survey (2017–18); US—ILOSTAT (2018)

When it comes to age, if the pattern of women's participation in the labour force in developed countries is plotted on a graph, the up–down–up–down curve it forms resembles an 'M' (at least in recent history).[2] This is the M–curve, and its utility is in providing an immediate glimpse of the ages women work, and the ages they don't. On a typical M–curve, the percentage of women's participation rises significantly for women in their twenties, then falls in the years when they typically marry or have children. It rises again as women gradually resume work thereafter, and dips at retirement.

In India, of course, women's participation rates are dramatically lower across the board. They rise gradually until around the age of forty, and then more and more women drop out of the workforce permanently. India's M–curve resembles the head of an A–curve. (The incline and decline are so gentle that it would be more accurate to call it an 'a–curve'.) India doesn't just have a problem of bringing women into the workforce, but of ensuring that they stay the course.

It is important to keep in mind that half of Indian women are married by the age of nineteen. One in three women have had a child before the age of twenty.[3] In developed economies, anywhere between 50 and 80 per cent of women in the age group 25-35 join the workforce. India charts its own path: In that age group, only one in four women engage in paid work.

The M-Curve

Women's Labour Force Participation Rate by Age

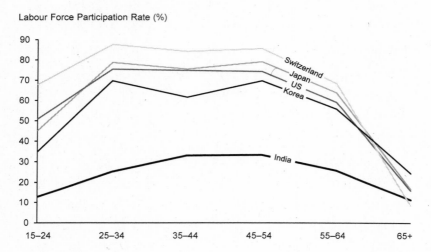

Labour Force Participation Rate (%)

Source: ILOSTAT (2018)

Why is the shape for India different when it comes to the U- and M-curves? During the course of our research, we came across diverse forces that play a major role in women not working. These forces are not unique to India, but the extent to which they play out is significant. Largely, they fall into three categories:

Unpaid Work

Women work, but aren't paid for their efforts. Data shows that Indian women are responsible for 87 per cent of unpaid care work—one of the highest shares in the world, far higher than China (at 72 per cent) and the US (at 61 per cent). This is the work of caring for children and elders, of managing a household. The magnitude of work cannot be overstated. In India, women perform 9.8 times as much care work as men. That is, for every hour of housework that men put in—cleaning, nurturing, cooking, teaching, advising, managing—women put in ten hours. This is another kind of a shadow economy; it demands work and sacrifice, but there's no pay cheque at the end of the month. If all this unpaid work were valued and compensated in the same way as paid work, it would contribute $300 billion to India's economic output.[4]

Safety and Mobility

More often than not, when Indian women decide to take up work, the calculation includes an additional item: The cost of safe travel. The habit starts even before work. College-going women in Delhi are willing to spend ₹18,000 ($257) more than men on safer commuting options annually. Women prefer attending less prestigious colleges if they can travel via a safer route. When it comes to work, one survey shows, a large number are willing to migrate for work, but they are outnumbered by those who feel unsafe being away from home.[5] According to the World Bank economist Girija Borker, 'women's willingness to pay for safety translates into a 20 per cent decline' in the salaries they could have earned after graduating college.

A typical educated, urban working woman with a child loses over 15 per cent of salary to the gender pay gap and about one-sixth to childcare. Her commute is more expensive than her male counterparts, because she chooses safer options like grabbing a taxi at night from the train station to her home, rather than walking.

For a woman, the act of working is an expensive one.

For Women, Work Is Expensive: A Stylized Example[6]

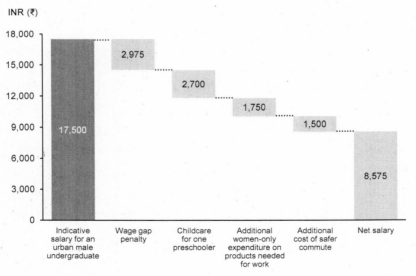

Source: Tata Sons and Dalberg analysis

Underlying Gender Norms

Gender expectations start early and can be borne out in census numbers: Between 2001 and 2011, India's child sex ratio further deteriorated from 927 girls to 919 girls for every thousand boys, reflecting a preference for sons.[7]

The reasons for son preference are far from uniform, and shift dramatically across regions and cultures. In some areas, traditions and norms leading to son preference include keeping property in the family, avoiding paying dowry, having support close at hand in parents' old age (daughters typically marry and move away), and because sons perform last rites. Even in matrilineal societies across the country, evidence for son preference can be found.

Expectations about gender roles play into routine daily activities. In a nationwide survey, 80 per cent of women said they needed permission from a family member to visit a health centre and 58 per cent needed permission to visit the local *kirana* (grocery) store.[8] Without the freedom of movement to conduct everyday tasks, discussing the opportunities of doing paid work away from home takes on new heights.

These three broad sets of interwoven issues—unpaid work, safety and mobility, and underlying gender norms—have deep roots, but sometimes it takes just one outlier, like a determined woman in Punjab, to upend notions of what seems possible.

16

Waiting for a Role Model

It took a while for Manbir to convince his mother, who initially had reservations about her daughter-in-law working. A woman working outside her home goes against tradition in Punjab's rural areas. 'While my father had no problem with Jasleen working in the formal sector, many neighbours and relatives raised a problem. I had to make my mother understand that with Jasleen working as a government employee, it would not only help us financially, but would also help our children and family on the whole, and raise our standard in society,' he said.

His conviction bore fruit. Because of Jasleen's work, their household income had grown to more than ₹50,000 ($714) every month. Their kitchen had an electric chimney and a blender, tea was served in elegant bone china, the floor was tiled in marble, and the house was undergoing an expansion for the children.

When Jasleen joined the police, Manbir said, the news came as a shock to the villagers. 'They said, "She's in such a big job? Because of her education?" They came to congratulate us.' The sweetest outcome of Jasleen's success was that villagers decided to educate their own daughters and daughters-in-law. Following Jasleen's lead, between fifteen and twenty girls from the village started to attend college. The school's principal sought her out to speak to students. And young women constantly asked her for career advice.

Jasleen's daughter had watched her work, and decided that she too would work one day. Hardeep, Jasleen's father-in-law, took care of the children, while his wife cooked breakfast and lunch. Manbir said that Jasleen's long hours meant there was little time to catch up. 'You know these police personnel can be called away at any time. They work twenty-four hours a day. And she's doing a very big job at such a young age.'

Jasleen planned to educate her children without worrying about where the money would come from. Whatever their education cost them, she and Manbir decided, they wouldn't compromise. 'I will let them study and even send them for higher professional education if they wish, when the time comes,' she said.

The circle was virtuous. She wanted the children to move outside the state for their higher education. Achieving dreams required the kind of exposure found only in top colleges and universities. 'I will ensure that my children get quality education and do not suffer like I did due to poverty. Education is the most important aspect of life where one not only becomes literate, but also finds friends and well-wishers, and understands what life actually is,' Jasleen said. Manbir Singh nodded in agreement.

17

Releasing the Talent Gridlock

In a dusty corner of the country, a woman in a village quietly slips out of her home to attend digital literacy classes because her father or husband have forbidden it. When she learns to send messages and take pictures, the phone is declared a corrupting influence. In Delhi, a college student moves to a new home to avoid bus 544 and the men it contains. During a job interview, an executive from human resources asks a candidate when she intends on getting pregnant. Elsewhere, marriage bureaus reassure families that their daughter's degree qualifies them for a discount on dowry payments. After work, women share stories about certain men. Phone manufacturers advertise a new feature for women: Emergency buttons. In earnest, a business report's researcher declares that men are biologically incapable of maintaining relationships the way women can, and declares that is why companies must value women. The simple act of walking on a busy street is as stressful at forty-two as it is at twelve.

To understand the problem of women's participation in the workforce, we spoke to cooperatives, start-ups, politicians, students, some of India's largest companies, businesses which run women-only shop floors, firms that struggled to hire any women at all, women running hiring platforms, rural men and women engaged in informal work, Ivy-League-educated women who are out of work, researchers, women in the south, north, east, west, north-east and abroad.

There's no simple playbook to ease the tall, invisible barriers that keep women from work. Countries around the world are grappling with these questions in different ways. The US, for example, has witnessed declining rates of work participation by women after generations of improvement.[1]

Many policy examples abound. Austria lowered the income tax on second earners to encourage women's participation in the labour force; Belgium mandated organizations (with over fifty employees) to conduct a gender pay gap analysis every two years and produce an action plan to tackle pay inequality; the Philippines directed a minimum of 5 per cent of the national budget to gender and development initiatives. In Rwanda, investment in clean water provision freed up time for girls to go to school instead of spending substantial amounts of time fetching water. The country also has the most female parliamentarians in the world, after passing laws to ensure women's representation at all levels of governance.

We can take inspiration from a wealth of successful interventions that have taken place globally, as well as within India. Three focus areas address the issues that matter most.

Context is key. No other country is like India. Implementing these ideas will need to account for the vast diversity of roles and experiences women face. This will take time. But given what's at stake, the case for starting this journey today could not be clearer.

SOLUTION 1: BUILD A LEADING-EDGE TWENTY-FIRST-CENTURY CARE ECONOMY

In a central Mumbai skyscraper, a highly qualified group of women settled in at the building's private clubhouse to share what had stopped them from working. Several of them had an Ivy League education. Most of them were no longer part of the workforce. One, a chartered accountant, had a supportive husband, but her in-laws disapproved of her returning to work after the birth of her first child. Another said, 'Flexibility at the workplace is only in writing—nobody truly encourages it.' At one job interview, she was asked outright if she planned on having a second child. 'There is a reason why there are more male CXOs in the world,' she shrugged.

113

A third—a former management consultant—thought she would return to work three months after having a baby. But plans changed. 'I looked for a long time, but I just couldn't find a competent and consistent nanny.'

A thriving economy of care centres for children as well as older people, crèches, and domestic helpers can offer options for women who want and need to pursue careers. It also creates millions of new jobs.

There are as many models of the care economy as there are countries. Sweden's childcare system offers affordable day care and paid leave which parents can choose to share. Much of the system's success is because Sweden subsidizes costs and rewards quality. Private care providers receive public funding only if they follow national quality guidelines. This has increased and standardized the quality of services offered by providers throughout the country. No household has to pay more than 3 per cent of its income as childcare fees, raising low-income families' access to care. Single mothers from low-income backgrounds now do 16.5 per cent more paid work as a result. It turns out that kids who go to day care display better cognitive skills and psychological health.[2]

Mexico's Day Care Support for Working Mothers programme has community-based care providers and covers up to 90 per cent of the cost of childcare for women who work, want to work, or are studying. By 2018, nearly 10,000 centres served about 330,000 children. The programme increased the proportion of beneficiary mothers who were employed by 18 per cent and the average number of hours they worked each week increased by six. It also generated more than 40,000 paid jobs for providers and aides, most of whom were women.[3]

India can be even more ambitious. Examples of high-quality affordable care services within the country already abound. Mobile Creches, an NGO started in 1969, provides childcare facilities to communities underserved by government. The facilities are established on construction sites for migrant workers, whose assignments tend to be transient. They also serve residents of the area. In 2017–18, the organization provided childcare services to almost 11,000 children through its day-care programme and trained about 400 childcare workers. Among the testimonies they cite is one by the mother of a three-year-old child. It is filled with relief: 'Earlier, my attention was divided, [but now] I am able to focus on my sewing and doubling my earnings.'[4]

The benefits trickle down from mothers. When children were enrolled in community day-care centres (*Balwadis*) in Rajasthan for prolonged periods, they showed gains in nutrition, hygiene, cognition and school readiness skills.[5]

There are countless stories and testimonies, one more powerful than the next, but they only reaffirm what has been plain to see for years. When reassuring caregiving options are made available, everybody benefits. The Bank of Tokyo-Mitsubishi UFJ in Japan saw this first-hand with more than a fourfold increase in the retention of new mothers and saving an estimated $45 million in employee turnover after it offered childcare and extended maternity leave.[6]

Why should India invest heavily in the care sector? Because the interest is compounded. The work of the Nobel prize-winning economist James Heckman shows that early childhood care leads to some of the highest returns on any investments governments can make. It has immediate and long-term benefits through reductions in the need for special education and remediation; better health outcomes; reduced need for social services; lower criminal justice costs; and increased self-sufficiency and productivity among families. Conversely, a lack of investments in childcare during early years ends up creating deficits in skills and abilities, and inevitably drives down overall productivity, adding heavy financial costs to countries in the long run.[7]

By some estimates, the combined senior and childcare market in India is currently worth just $8 billion—less than a fifth of the size of the US market for day care alone. Yet India has four times the size of the US's dependent population. Its need for formal care support is greater. If India focused on childcare alone, it could create up to four million new jobs in the care industry—of which the vast majority would go to women—and help up to 10 million additional women participate in the workforce.[8]

In Europe, Women's Employment Rates Are Higher in Countries Where Family-Friendly Policies Are in Place

Women's Employment Rates by Region and Number of Children in Europe

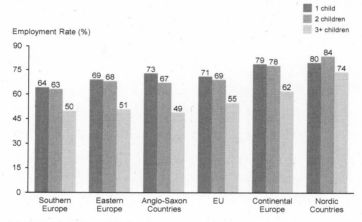

Note: Family policy regime classification:
Southern Europe: Limited assistance to families
Eastern Europe: Long leave but low cash benefits and childcare for children under the age of three
Anglo-Saxon countries: Paid leave period is short, with support targeted to low-income, single-parent families and families with preschool children
Continental Europe: High financial support, but limited service provision to support dual-earner families with children under the age of three
Nordic countries: Continuous, strong support for working parents of children under the age of three
Employment rate here refers to persons of age fifteen-plus who are employees, self-employed and family workers
Source: UN Women (2015)

The bigger challenge is to end the stigma of outsourcing care. Despite the advantages, the number of Indian families who use childcare is insignificant. One of the big reasons for this is the guilt associated with outsourcing care. Women would like to work, but are reluctant to outsource care out of fear that children and elders might feel isolated or estranged, and that, in general, it's not a good look.[9]

There are ways to work around this. In Japan—where, like in India, people are expected to care for their parents into older age—community-based or home-based day-care services for seniors are popular alternatives to full-time residential care. Karnataka has its Grama Hiriyara Kendras, care-centres that feed and look after senior citizens four hours a day, with helpers trained in geriatric care. There are early indications of growing social acceptance of the Kendras.[10]

It will take generations to undo the stigma around using carers outside the home. To speed this up, there needs to be clear evidence that the solution works in practice.

Users want quality. Professionalizing the sector will help. Families will want to know that their children and elderly parents are looked after by qualified staff in safe, high-quality facilities. Industry-wide accredited training and professional standards can help do this. Sweden's example also shows how the government can step in to further encourage private providers to deliver quality services. If the care economy is to grow sustainably into a dynamic and productive sector, the four million jobs that could be created need to be good jobs, where employees are protected and can carry out their work with dignity.

Bridgital solutions can signal a professional approach, which in turn would help undo the stigma associated with outsourcing care. For instance, childcare workers—whether attached to a care-centre or standalone—could be integrated into a cloud-based management system which allows them to do administrative tasks like reporting attendance, health and safety records, and also to undergo training. This would also enable real-time check-ins and scheduling, and offer a source of collaboration amongst parents. Moreover, individuals can also create a transferable professional history by adopting this platform-based approach, deepening their integration into the formal economy.

SOLUTION 2: ADDRESS UNINTENDED CONSEQUENCES THROUGH SMART GENDER POLICY

Well-intentioned policies can have unintentional outcomes. When India addressed women's safety concerns by restricting them from working at night in mines and beedi factories, all this did was reduce the number of hours women could work.[11] There could have been other ways to address safety risks: requiring companies to provide better and safer transportation, constant monitoring, and other infrastructure. Instead, for a factory owner deciding between hiring a man and a woman, the choice was a simple one: men could work at night, while women couldn't.

Policy intent also needs to translate into outcomes on the ground. A case in point is gender budgeting—a 'gender lens' in the process of budgeting for planning, formulation and implementation stages of nationwide policies. The Indian government adopted gender budgeting in 2005, yet there remains a gap between budgetary outlay and utilization of the allocated funds. A recent example is the low use (less than 20 per cent) by states of the budget allocated to them under the Nirbhaya Fund for women's safety between 2015 and 2018.[12] Earmarking certain funds is one thing, but making sure those funds are put to proper use is another.

India's Maternity Bill. When India introduced the Maternity Bill in 2017, it was hailed as one of the most progressive legislations of its kind anywhere. The Bill gives expectant and new mothers paid leave for six months. It also mandated that all workplaces of more than fifty employees provide access to crèche facilities.

But the Bill is complicated.

First, by providing working mothers with six months maternity leave but fathers with none, it reinforces the norm that raising children is women's work. (Countries sensitive to such policy signalling—mostly Nordic countries and Asian countries like South Korea and Japan—strongly encourage working fathers to take time off, even making it mandatory in some cases.)

120

Second, employers in India end up bearing the costs of implementing the Bill's provisions—providing paid leave, as well as crèche facilities. This discourages them from hiring women. Small and medium enterprises, in particular, struggle with this. The director of an instruments manufacturing firm told us that his company's head of human resources recommended hiring men and 'keeping down female headcount' after the Bill was introduced. 'She recommended we recruit only women who were past a certain age,' he said. This way the company could limit the Bill's cost implications.

The interpretation of the Bill is itself a source of confusion. The same firm had to seek legal advice to understand whether it had to provide crèche facilities on exceeding fifty women employees, or fifty employees, irrespective of gender. Well-meaning laws that don't account for the cost of their implementation encourage dismal creativity.

We could consider how the costs can be subsidized, especially considering that different financing models for maternity and parental leave have yielded positive results across the world. Employers solely pay for maternity benefits in a quarter of 185 countries, and combinations of funds from employers and the government finance maternity benefits in 16 per cent of countries.[13]

Aside from this, the scope of the law arguably could be wider. The law currently covers formal employers, and the crèche provision applies to firms with more than fifty employees. Many Indians still lack access to decent childcare options, such as parents working at employers of less than fifty people, as well as the many more informal workers. Laws supporting primary caregivers for elderly parents or in-laws could be introduced too.[14]

On average, high-income countries offer working mothers about four months' leave, but in some cases this is as high as twelve. In most of these countries, they receive at least two-thirds of full-time pay while on leave. The most progressive country policies have placed more emphasis on the question of which parent should get leave. Iceland offers nine months—three each for the mother and father and a further three for the parents to divide as they choose. In Sweden, if parents share time off, they receive tax credits. The combination of financial incentives, creative approaches to flexible work options, and tax and pension credits more than doubled the amount of paternity leave Swedish men took. And every month they take off boosts their partner's salary four years later by 7 per cent.[15]

Revisiting the Equal Remuneration Act. Both the UK and India have legislations which mandate equal pay for equal work. In 2017, the UK went a step further to correct for gender bias by requiring a disclosure of pay gaps from large employers (250 or more employees). In the second year of its implementation, about 44 per cent of employers noted an improvement in the pay gap from the previous year.[16] India can also look at ways to deepen and sharpen the implementation of the Equal Remuneration Act, its own equal pay for equal work legislation, introduced way back in 1976.

SOLUTION 3: AMPLIFY THE COUNTER-NARRATIVE

The opportunities Indian women have are limited by widespread notions of what men and women are better at. These distinctions are deeply ingrained across every strata of society, and they turn up in surprising ways.

Some years ago, a renowned architect known for his use of natural materials was working on a commission east of Mumbai. He decided to pay men and women onsite the same wage. In his opinion, both the men and women were equally contributing to the overall project. The workers were locals and mostly married couples. For women, this meant an increase in their earnings.

However, the architect and the firm did not bargain for opposition. The workers, both men and women, were outraged and protested against the proposed hike. Then the local panchayat, headed by a woman, also joined the protest. Years later, the architect was still confounded by what had happened. He said the protests were called off only when the old wages were reinstated.

But there was more to the episode. The women workers were under the impression that equal pay meant taking on more physically taxing work. It didn't occur to them that their existing work merited better pay. Contractors and workers said that although the hike was well-intentioned, it could have led to 'uprisings' across construction sites nearby because 'rates were pre-decided' and any move to change existing practices was unthinkable.

There are ways to move past this.

Start early. The younger they are, greater the opportunity to change attitudes. NGOs like Breakthrough, which focus on women's and children's rights, have already shown that gender equality classes in school can make a bigger difference than other women's empowerment schemes, such as cash transfers. Girls exposed to these types of gender equality classes are likely to have more bargaining power in household decisions and delay marriage and childbirth. Boys who attended these classes helped out more with cooking and cleaning at home.[17]

In Haryana, school interventions by Breakthrough led to the start of a virtuous cycle. Filled with confidence, girls from one school formed collectives. They successfully convinced reluctant neighbours to send their daughters to school. The girls enlisted the village leader, who reassured parents that a school-going daughter was in their best interest. To the parents' initial horror and eventual delight, their daughters began playing sports traditionally considered male-oriented, such as kabaddi.

Also, education boards can remove content from textbooks that reinforces negative stereotypes. School textbooks in India are riddled with stories and pictures that paint men as breadwinners and women in passive roles, or depictions of gender roles at home like that of a mother cutting vegetables in the kitchen, while the father reads a newspaper. One textbook went further, stating that women's employment was 'a cause of rising unemployment' in the country. A small number of states are waking up to this issue. Education boards in Karnataka and Tamil Nadu now have textbooks that depict women with careers and all family members sharing in housework.

What's needed, at all levels, is nuance and imagination. 'You may have learned one thing at school in terms of gender justice, but may have to completely go against that at home because of social conditioning,' Arti Nair, a teacher, says. 'That's why it's essential for students to know that they are all part of the same system and must find ways of engaging with it in their own individualized ways.'

Magnify experiences that break the mould. Such stories involve women like Supriya Tambe, the first woman to obtain an assistant electrician diploma at a pan-India vocational skills initiative.[18] Supriya found the experience alienating at first, but as she persevered and grew in confidence, her fellow classmates became her biggest cheerleaders. The idea of a woman electrician didn't seem unusual to her or her peers any more. There are now more women in the same certification programme. Sneha, the head of a women's self-help group in Mumbai, said, 'Women at the grass-roots level need relatable role models. They don't care about a woman chief of a global bank. They don't relate to that. But if we succeed in drawing one woman from her own community, out of her home and into a profession, she serves as a role model for so many others. That helps in changing mindsets towards women working.'

If we can make a wider range of viable jobs both aspirational and accessible to women, and foster role models in sectors where they are under-represented, it will go a long way in opening up more avenues for gainful work.

Industry-level collaboration and targeted platforms can help prepare the ground for gender-balance. Slowly but steadily, we have seen employers devising new ways to address gender issues at work. For instance, upon entering India, IKEA publicly pledged to build an equitable workplace for everyone. They started by ensuring that more women operated warehouse forklifts.[19] Industry and CEO forums could also enable firms to make the commitment to gender equality more concrete, if top leadership pushes for practical steps towards rethinking talent, and redesigning work and workplaces accordingly.

Second, we can strengthen and scale digital platforms that help create a marketplace for women seeking jobs. These platforms can promote better targeting and matching of jobs, based on job preferences expressed by women. These steps would induce and support greater formalization of work.

We can't overstate the importance of these measures, led by firms and industries in the formal sector. While women have been leaving the workforce in aggregate, formal sector jobs are the exception. Over the period between 2011 and 2017, the share of women (versus men) in formal jobs rose to 26 per cent from 19 per cent, against a drop in women's share of informal work from 28 per cent to 22 per cent.[20] Building on this momentum, and better understanding the link between formal jobs and women's participation in India is key.

Entrepreneurship could also prove a fruitful bridge to paid work. Indonesia is an Asian success story: Women own more than half of all micro, small and medium enterprises (MSMEs). In India, this figure is lower than 14 per cent. Digital platforms expand possibilities even further, allowing quick and low-cost access to global markets for small-scale and growing ventures. In Indonesia, the share of women-owned MSMEs in e-commerce revenue is 35 per cent compared with only 15 per cent offline.[21]

The Bridgital approach, coupled with an enabling ecosystem for entrepreneurship, would not just create more jobs, but better jobs.

18

The Easiest Fix

We have what it takes to get started today—a huge store of untapped talent and skill, from potential electricians to skyscrapers filled with women with highly specialized qualifications who dream of finding a way back to a career. Twenty-six per cent of women with medical graduate degrees and 46 per cent of those with diplomas or vocational training degrees are out of the workforce—far higher than the figures for men.[1] Making work work for Indian women is paramount; this is a rare chance for India to go beyond statements of intent and prove that it truly wants more inclusive growth.

We've done it in letter and by law. It's time we did it in spirit.

The Jobs Challenge

19

Puzzles

It was lunchtime. Bhoomi and her friends were in the school canteen, joking about the okra and beetroot on their trays. They played with the vegetables using a spoon, delaying the inevitable. Teachers would soon come along to chat with the students, but they fooled no one: Everyone knew they were really making sure the food didn't go to waste.

The young women had been talking shop. Their Global Perspectives class, a crowd favourite in the tenth grade, let each student choose their own research topic. Bhoomi's topic had frustrated her. She had originally chosen to answer whether economic development was more important than human development, but after researching the topic for a month and a half, a satisfying answer still eluded her.

She decided, then, to understand the various effects of urbanization. 'Everybody says that urbanization is good and cities are where the job opportunities are. But there are negative impacts too, and not just on the environment. It also affects mental health, and affects relationships between people.' Her friends agreed, and she went on, making an example of herself. 'I have a much broader perspective now than if I had stayed back in the village.'

'What do you mean?' Janvi, her friend, asked. 'We need evidence!' she said, echoing their teacher's favourite line.

'Okay fine,' Bhoomi said, laughing. 'If I still lived in the village, I wouldn't have known that psychology was a science. I wouldn't have known that people studied the human mind and how people behave.'

Bhoomi was thirteen when she left her village in Karnataka for the faraway big city of Pune. She only knew Kannada—the language she had heard the farmers around her speak. Pune was filled with the sounds of Marathi, Hindi and English—all of which were alien to her. She left before the sixth standard, the year Hindi is introduced in Karnataka. As for English, she knew the basics, like 'A is for Apple'.

The city was primed to help her. When Bhoomi arrived, a movement to reform Pune's educational system was already under way. Non-profits and the local government had come together in unprecedented collaboration to improve the quality of education for every student in the city. She enrolled in a residential secondary school for girls with academic and leadership potential. Her brother attended a charter school at the other end of the city. They quickly became known as talented student-athletes. At the same time, the range of languages she understood expanded.

Bhoomi's classmates came from all over India, but what really bound them was that they were all the children of urban workers in India's vast informal sector. Their parents were rickshaw drivers, construction workers, vegetable sellers, domestic workers, and tailors. Bhoomi's parents ran a vegetable stall an hour away from the school.

Bhoomi opted to live in the school dorm during the week. Her family's home, a space 12 feet wide and just as long, bustled with parents and teenage brothers. The quiet time she needed to prepare for her tenth-grade exams—the terror of children and parents alike—was next to impossible. At home, there were always other demands on her time. Someone would catch her reading textbooks and rope her into managing the vegetable stall at night. This meant going to bed after midnight, and making time to study before everyone woke up.

During the week at the hostel, she grabbed time to study, but it never seemed enough. Still, she seemed confident. 'As long as I get enough time, I can do well.' The bell rang and her friends got up to wash their trays, giving her last-minute encouragement on their way out.

When they left, Bhoomi spoke more freely. 'I get discouraged at home sometimes. I'm excited and want to share things that I'm learning, but they tell me to keep it to myself.' This was partly why she preferred to live in the school dorm. She lived with the persistent expectations of family members who were torn between the distant benefits of good schooling, and the immediate need for extra hands. 'On the one hand it's my tenth-grade year and I have to focus. On the other hand, my mind is not free to focus. At the hostel, I am free to study, but I feel guilty being away from home. If I were there, I could help my mother or maybe ease some of the tension that's in the house.'

She didn't know what to choose. 'Work? Or education? I have to do both! If there were no debts, there would be no conflict. There is a puzzle right in front of my family, and we can't figure out how to get out of it. I feel like I know how to open the lock, but I am not able to use the key.'

Despite the confidence she projected with her friends, Bhoomi was not sure that she could continue with school once her exams were done the following month.

20

Jobs Count

Bhoomi is one of 90 million who will join India's working-age population between 2020 and 2030. This will be the single largest mass of people to come of working age in any country that decade. They will play an important role at a pivotal time—when other large economies will collectively see a reduction in their working-age populations, led by China. What India does will be crucial to the future of work globally.[1]

This generation of subcontinental millennials and Gen Z-ers is charged with lifting India from poverty to middle-income status, exactly what the generation currently in its fifties did for China.[2] But to replicate China's success, India will have to prepare the ground for its citizens to find productive work.

India: The World's Emerging Workforce

Additions to Working Age Population between 2020 and 2030 for the Ten Largest Economies

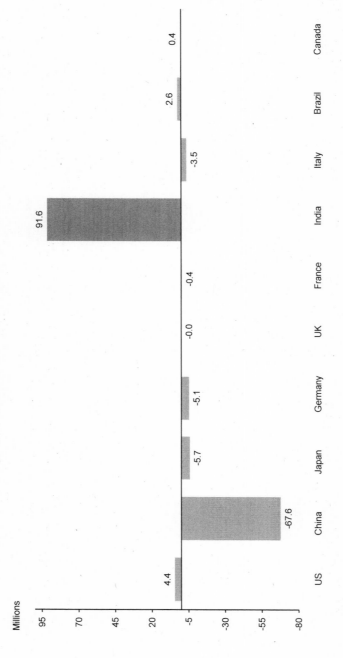

Millions

Note: Countries from left to right, in decreasing order of 2018 nominal GDP
Working age is assumed to be 15 to 59 years

Source: IMF's World Economic Outlook Database (2019); UN DESA (2019)

As it stands, the labour market they enter has three distinguishing characteristics. First, it brims with people of working age, but who are not necessarily part of the labour force.[3] Second, those seeking work will find it more challenging than in previous decades. Third, of those that find jobs, an overwhelming number will be engaged in work that is of an informal nature.

Let's look at these three essential aspects.

The first is that a large number of people who could work are not looking for work.

To gauge the labour market, people often turn to a country's unemployment rate. They may believe the figure represents a portion of the working-age population. That is, they may believe that India's 6 per cent unemployment rate is for a population of 970 million.[4]

But analysts and statisticians assess unemployment differently. The official rate represents a portion of only those people who want to work—those actually working, or in the process of looking for work. It hides from view the people who aren't looking for work at all.

This wouldn't matter much in a country where almost everyone of working-age was looking to work. In India, though, only around 450 million people had jobs and 29 million others were seeking work as of 2017. In other words, a little less than one in two working-age people were actually working, or looking for work. By comparison, three in four people in China have been working (or actively seeking work), on average, since the 1990s.[5]

That leaves nearly 490 million people of working age outside the bounds of India's unemployment assessments. That is why India's unemployment could be misunderstood. A decrease in the unemployment rate could signal economic growth, but could just as well mean that people have given up looking for work.

Who are these people left so unaccounted that India doesn't know they're missing? Who are these millions of Indians who have quit or never even joined the labour force? We know for certain that a large number of them are women. Only 23 per cent of all women who can work are part of the labour force, while for men, the figure is about 75 per cent.

Some people choose to remain in school. For others, the jobs are too far away. India's northern and eastern states have the highest population growth rates and large youth populations, while the jobs these restless young seek in manufacturing and services are concentrated in states in the south and the west.

There are others who have given up on looking for work. They have tried finding jobs that match their needs and aspirations, and failed. And the longer they spend out of work, the harder it becomes to find any job at all. These are the discouraged workers.

The second characteristic of the labour market is a rising unemployment rate.

For the past two decades, India's unemployment rate has hovered in the 2–3 per cent range. Most people looking for a job were able to land one. However, in 2017, the unemployment rate rose to 6 per cent. While still not alarmingly high, it is important to look below the surface. For some critical groups, unemployment—the onerous search for a job—is a matter of greater concern.

For young people between the ages of fifteen and twenty-nine, the unemployment rate is nearly 18 per cent. When it comes to urban, tertiary educated people, the unemployment rate is 12–15 per cent. For Bhoomi and her friends, the jobs landscape is a more treacherous one than they are led to believe. They will face difficult choices on the cusp of entering the workforce. Should they invest in higher education, only to join the ranks of the unemployed? Or are that time and effort better spent on trying to earn what they can? How long should they hold out on getting a job that fits their vision of the future? Should they prioritize some, any employment over none at all? To them, the India of the senses feels a lot closer than the India of the numbers, and families like Bhoomi's make decisions deeply aware that the stakes are high.[6]

The third characteristic: Overwhelmingly, those who join the workforce tend to find jobs in the low-productivity informal sector.

This is not India's first rodeo when it comes to absorbing large numbers of people into the workforce. From the turn of the century through 2011, India added 76 million workers to its workforce. However, the majority of these jobs were informal jobs; 77 per cent of India's employed are currently in the informal sector.[7]

The informal sector is a world of work that exists in grey. Everything one can say about the informal sector is an approximation. Even definitions of the term paint a picture of imprecision. It is unregistered, unorganized, without contracts, social security, a regular salary, or an assured volume of work. Seen another way, if the economy were an iceberg, the informal side would be hidden beneath the water surface, encompassing a huge range of occupations. Farming and construction would be among them. So would car repair shops, traders, shop-owners, textile workers and beedi rollers.[8]

Decades of research show that informal work is characterized by high risk, and virtually no systems of insurance, regulation or safety standards.

Most of all, it is marked by low productivity.[9]

Many who work in the informal sector can be more accurately described as 'underemployed'. They are less productive and lower-paid than workers in the formal sector. In fact, they may earn as little as half of what organized, formal workers earn per day of work. The bulk earn less than ₹11,000 ($160) a month.[10]

Meanwhile, because formal businesses learn and spread management procedures, protocols and best practices, they're in a better position to realize the benefits of investing in technology and assets to upgrade their production processes. This can spark a virtuous cycle of productivity and growth for a business.

In turn, they are incentivized to invest in their employees, who form the other crucial part of the productivity equation. Workers in a labour market with more formal opportunities see greater job stability as well as expanded future job prospects; a legal and regulatory framework; sanctity of contracts; workplace standards and streamlined access to credit.

India's great search for work is really about a pursuit of stable work in the formal sector. It is a goal for which India's young go to extremes.

For two hours every morning and evening, over a thousand students assemble on the Sasaram train station platform in Bihar to prepare for their competitive examinations. The *station-waale ladke* (station boys), as they're known, travel from distant areas to study under the station's lamp posts—the station being the one public space with uninterrupted electricity. All of them hope to find government jobs—prized for the security they provide—after passing their exams.

There is no dearth of lamp-post students in India, and competition for each job is intense. For the contenders who miss out, a life in the informal sector awaits. In comparison to these students, Bhoomi is one of the few facing the jobs landscape with decent preparation, but the odds are still stacked against her.

Her Global Perspectives research may not have gone as planned, but even in this seeming failure, Bhoomi's insight reflects her stubborn wisdom. 'To be frank, everyone in class says human development is more important, but a country like ours needs economic development—they both go hand in hand. I don't see a way around it.' It wasn't clear whether she arrived at this more from the month and a half of futile research, or her own life experience. Probably a bit of both.

21

Waterproof

When the drought of 2003 came, and the village land could no longer provide for his family, Bhoomi's father, Rajappa Biyali, began to consider his only real option, a life in India's cities. What else could he do? The sky above Mannur was his, and five acres of its ground were his, but what good were these without rain? He could not experiment with his crops, much less grow sesame and toovar (lentils) the way he desired.

The district, which lay at the border of the states of Karnataka and Maharashtra, did not offer much to the industrious. It is one of the most underdeveloped places in the region. There was little to do but farm. The drought took away that work too. Before long, Rajappa began to walk in the footsteps of many before him, guided by a future he could only imagine.

Rajappa had studied until the eleventh grade, and only dropped out when his family could not afford to pay for his education. On an uncle's beckoning, he travelled to Pune and joined him as a construction worker. Many new building projects were under way in 2004. The city had witnessed an influx of blue-collar workers, information technology professionals, and students. The construction business there needed people like Rajappa, people who undertook gruelling work without question for ₹150 ($2) a day.

Across the country, the construction industry's promise of a steady income and demand for labour attracted Rajappa and millions of other farm workers giving up agriculture. There were so many of them that construction labourers came to form one of the country's largest employee bases, absorbing more lapsed farm workers than any other sector.

For Rajappa, city life meant a better wage, but making do with less in other ways. He could not speak Hindi, the language of construction sites, and had to teach himself this new language on the job. Home was a small makeshift tin shed beside the construction site. At night he dreamed of his fields, the smell of the soil, and, above all, his children. He clutched at the memories of his land, and when he finally bought a mobile phone, he carried pictures of his fields as someone would keep photographs of family.

He visited home every other month, but it was never enough. The children—Bhoomi, Bijay and Saju—sprang

146

new words and new behaviours. He reminded himself why he was so far from them. It was important to keep his head in the work. Around him, workers took to drink and drugs. Rajappa assessed many of them as more talented than him, but they preferred intoxication.

Within a year, Rajappa had picked up Hindi and became proficient at construction techniques. 'I watched and learned. I settled quickly,' he said. He became a small foreman, leading a group of labourers, training them and giving them instructions. Now he watched others carry construction supplies across the site. Moving further up the hierarchy of construction required specialization. There were jobs to be had on each building site, but they were 'a lot of hard labour and little money'.

In 2007, he calculated that his future was in waterproofing. The trade was the opposite of most construction site jobs. 'It has less work for more profits,' he said. Life had turned Rajappa into an accountant, constantly measuring the cash flows of survival. Rajappa devoured books and manuals, hungry to understand how waterproofing worked. He fabricated a pump to spray mixes into floors and crevices. 'Not everyone has the know-how and can do it well.'

There was another reason Rajappa decided on the trade. Over a metre of rain had fallen in the region during each of the previous two years, and waterproofers were in great demand. In 2007, three years after Rajappa moved to the city, his wife, Sangamma, and his son, Saju, joined the family in their tiny city home. Demand for his services had picked up, and there were even inquiries from outside the state.

But the two years of heavy rain proved an aberration. In the first three years of his career as a waterproofer, rainfall in the region dropped substantially. Less rainfall meant fewer damp buildings, and fewer contracts. He chased after contractors for more work, and then chased after them to pay up. 'There have never been any guarantees,' he said. 'Pune or Mannur, I can't escape the rain.'

22

A Two-Track Economy

Although they aspire to greater security and steadiness, workers like Rajappa—talented, driven and industrious—are locked out of India's formal economy, which requires levels of education and skill beyond their reach. India's potential workers are largely educated only up to primary school, and only one in fifty have received any kind of formal vocational or skills training.[1]

In response to this concerning trend, a decade ago the country decided to focus on vocational training programmes. For instance, in recent years, at least 3 million people have been trained as tailors, welders, car mechanics, caretakers and mobile technicians, under the Pradhan Mantri Kaushal Vikas Yojana (PMKVY)—one of the flagship skills programmes. While progress has been made in addressing the fragmentation and lack of coordination that has long dogged skilling in India, it remains a challenge to achieve the scale needed. Several different ministries continue to run programmes in their respective areas, and a clear link to the demand for skills from employers is lacking. Qualified trainers are in short supply. Apprenticeships—recently reformed to be more employer-friendly—are still relatively rare. Of the millions trained, a little over half receive job offers.[2]

Herein lies India's jobs challenge—a very large number of working-age people need to find productive jobs that they can do at their *existing* levels of skill or education.

The figure on page 151 reveals why there is no easy way out of India's employment challenge. It maps the relative placement of key sectors of India's economy on two dimensions. The more productive the sector—that is, the greater the value of goods and services it produces (gross value added or GVA) per hour or day of workers' time—the higher it is in the chart, and the more its workers are likely to earn as wages. The more skill-intensive the sector—in other words, the higher the share of skilled workers in its total workforce—the further to the right it is placed. In the absence of any quantifiable measure of skill, we use the achievement of a secondary level of education as a stand-in.

In the bottom left quadrant, where most of India's workers are to be found, is the unorganized and informal economy, a place where few people have a secondary education. In the upper right quadrant are the fast-growing, high-productivity, organized sectors, which employ less than a quarter of the Indian workforce, but where up to 90 per cent of workers have a secondary education.[3]

Between them is a vast gap.

India's Challenge: Productive Employment Is Skill-Intensive, While the Workforce Is Not

Comparison of Productivity and Skill Intensity across Sectors of the Indian Economy in 2011–12

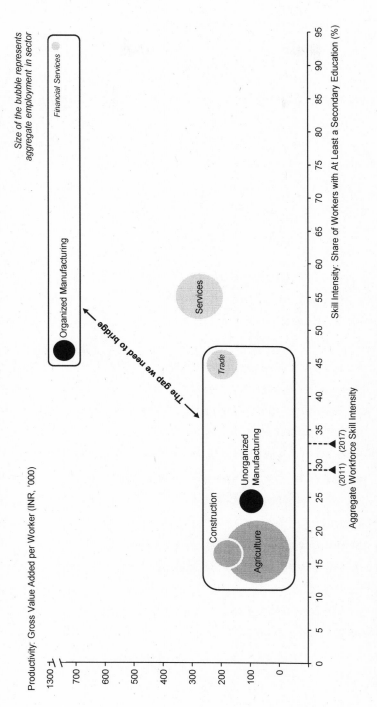

Productivity: Gross Value Added per Worker (INR, '000)

Size of the bubble represents aggregate employment in sector

Skill Intensity: Share of Workers with At Least a Secondary Education (%)

Aggregate Workforce Skill Intensity

The gap we need to bridge

Note: Employment estimations for organized manufacturing assume all firms with 10 or more employees as organized

Source: Tata Sons analysis; National Accounts Statistics 2011–12; NSSO 68th Round 2011–12

This is the larger force to which Rajappa is beholden. For him, construction was a step up from agriculture, but it's nowhere near the productivity level of a formal factory job. He does not have options in front of him that can act as stepping stones—or, for a more modern metaphor, escalators—to move from construction to more productive parts of the economy.

This reflects a country that runs on two tracks. At one end is the organized sector, intensely productive, well-paying, high-skilled, with fewer workers. Diagonally opposite is the unorganized sector, marked by large numbers of less qualified and lower-paid workers who add less value (per worker) to the economy.

The formal sector, meanwhile, has a different problem: Vacancies. There are over 5,800 vacant seats for judges; the vacancy rate for general physicians in the Indian public health system is over 32 per cent; elementary schools in Uttar Pradesh and Bihar need nearly 400,000 teachers. In the private sector, 56 per cent of employers say they find it difficult to fill vacant roles.[4] And even when those roles are filled, new hires undergo rigorous training programmes—the equivalent of another semester or even another year of education—to prepare them for work.

The lopsided employment scene is the reason why the act of job hunting has become a spectator sport in India.

India Has a Skewed Profile: Too Few Have Completed Secondary Education[5]

Educational Attainment across Developing Countries

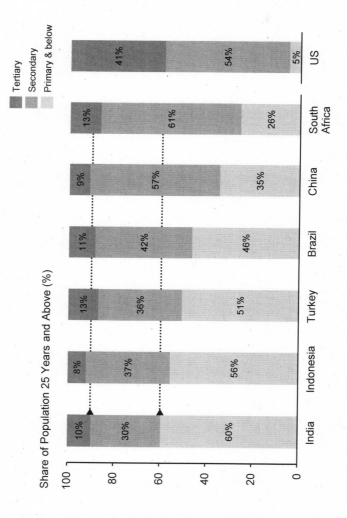

Share of Population 25 Years and Above (%)

	Tertiary	Secondary	Primary & below
India	10%	30%	60%
Indonesia	8%	37%	56%
Turkey	13%	36%	51%
Brazil	11%	42%	46%
China	9%	57%	35%
South Africa	13%	61%	26%
US	41%	54%	5%

Note: Data for different years: 2010—China; 2011—Brazil, Indonesia; 2012—India, South Africa, Turkey and the United States

Source: Institute for Human Development (2016); US Census Bureau (2012)

The fascination is with the spectacle of the large numbers India unleashes given the smallest of outlets, like a river bursting through a single tap. A recent news story highlighted the responses to a job posting announcing sixty-two messengers' job in the Uttar Pradesh police department. The role required applicants to have a primary school education and experience riding a bicycle. It paid ₹20,000 ($285) a month. More than 50,000 graduates, 28,000 postgraduates and 3,700 doctorates applied.[6] There are so many educated unemployed that they easily crowd workers with lower qualifications out of the clutch of secure jobs they could have found.

This situation has arisen partly because India invests heavily in tertiary education while not investing enough in primary and secondary education. As a result, the country's education profile is peculiar: Citizens tend to be either highly educated or minimally educated, with not many in between.

Given the low and inconsistent quality of educational outcomes, employability (or lack thereof) is a rampant issue. Facing workers with low employability and the need to invest in on-job training, employers struggle to offer jobs that match the aspirations of workers who have already invested substantially in their education by getting a college degree.

Government Spending Reflects the Tilt towards Tertiary Education[7]

Government Spending on Education across Countries 2005–15

Ratio of Spending: Tertiary to Primary Education

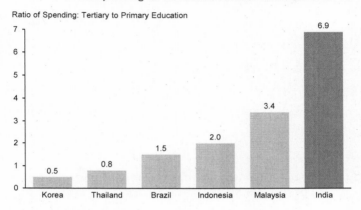

Note: Expenditure on primary and tertiary education is on per student basis
Source: UNESCO Institute for Statistics

Consequently, the economy grapples with human capital mismatches across the board. There are positions that remain vacant for lack of personnel who want to fill them, to mid-level roles held by underqualified workers, to highly skilled professionals who—while well-suited to their responsibilities—cannot achieve maximum productivity because they are occupied with tasks that could be done by others.

India cannot complete the critical work to build the nation and its economy when the country is hampered by an undersupply of proficient human capital and systemic misallocation of talent, with no ability to build a proper pipeline of high-calibre workers. The talent shortage is real,

155

resulting from a lack of access to relevant education and skills training, and it results in inadequate staffing up and down the employment spectrum.

One of the ways India can right this talent mismatch is by focusing on its secondary-educated workforce. The incremental impact of a secondary and higher-educated workforce on national growth tends to be greater for countries like India. These workers can become the technicians, sales executives, and customer service agents that will be needed as the middle class expands, but which might not meet the aspirations of a college-educated person. This isn't a new idea; we've seen it play out this way before. The 'Asian miracle' that led South Korea, Japan and Taiwan, among others, on the path of sustained high and equitable economic growth had more to do with investments in primary and secondary education than with investments in higher education.[8]

On the back of these experiences, India's secondary education strategy needs to centre on both raising the quality of educational outcomes and facilitating transitions for people with secondary education to the labour market.

For India, there is—at this moment—no clear path between informal and formal work, no road map to help people bridge the gap to prosperity. Its jobs landscape has a participation gap, a skills gap and a gap between the informal and formal sectors. We need to simultaneously ramp up skills, focus more on secondary education, and free up room for more employers to move informal work closer to the formal end of the spectrum. This is the key to India's jobs puzzle.

It's a high-wire act, given the time, and India will have to do more than just offer its citizens traditional vocational training in preparation for the future.

23

Twice Exposed

By 2012, the family was reunited in Pune. Bhoomi and Bijay left their grandparents and the village to join their parents and brother in the city. The change was as stark for them as it had been for Rajappa. For one, few of the locals spoke Kannada. Then there was the cramped room they called home. At night, the three siblings slept on the floor, half their bodies stretched out below their parents' bed. They learned to check how much water was left in the blue barrel in the alley outside—their sole source of water for the day— and to make sure never to miss the water delivery man when he came by to refill it.

The year his family came together again, Rajappa was cutting through a wall with a power saw when the blade jammed and splintered, slashing his right hand. He was rushed to a hospital nearby: it was one he had helped waterproof, and some of the staff knew him. When Sangamma arrived, her husband was on a stretcher. His hand would require surgery. The cost of the operation was ₹50,000 ($715). The family's savings could not cover these expenses; a neighbour loaned her the money after Sangamma promised to repay twice the amount over twenty months. She later recalled there was no time to think about the heavy cost of the loan.

The day after the surgery, Rajappa returned to work. 'The doctor asked me to rest at home for a week. What a joke! Who has that kind of time?' he wondered. It did not matter if he could effectively use his hand. He always had the other one. He was more troubled by the terms of the loan, which were beyond anything he could earn. Rajappa took a bank loan to repay the neighbour. The interest rate was 8.5 per cent, far lower than the absurd rate their neighbour had charged, but he soon fell behind on those repayments as well.

A precarious financial existence begets unexpected entanglements. The emergency loan for the surgery wasn't the first of these. There were agricultural loans to repay for bore wells Rajappa had built back home. He had never quite managed to leave agriculture behind—he had hoped that proper irrigation with the borewells might just turn his family's luck around. But as of now, he only had the loans to show.

Then there were the moneylenders, who came by to collect their 3 per cent interest every month. There was also the matter of being the eldest son, a responsibility that meant he sometimes had to shoulder his siblings' financial obligations.

Six years after his accident, Rajappa earned ₹20,000 ($285) in a good month—two-thirds more than the average Indian's monthly income.[1] Yet the family struggled with poverty. His debts had ballooned to ₹550,000 ($7,850), more than two and a half times their yearly income. Whichever way Rajappa looked at the debt situation, a permanent solution was never in sight.

To pay the price for raising three teenagers, meeting household expenses, managing the rent, and avoiding defaulting on bank payments, the Biyali household juggled its finances endlessly. They prioritized one lender one month, another the next, always working for a sum that never felt enough. 'We live with this constant pressure,' Rajappa said. The agricultural loans in Karnataka and the debt in Pune had left him twice exposed.

24

Escalator Sectors

India does not resemble the traditional story analysts tell about economic progress.

In that story, an economy grows as more people work to produce more goods and services. People move from farms to factories. Labour is more productive, even if it isn't more educated or skilled. The additional income this generates over time lets families invest in better standards of living—better housing, more nutritious food—as well as better education for their children. This better-educated generation then take up even more skilled and specialized roles, including in services like healthcare, scientific research, and finance and investment.

It is a story of growth.

Looking at India's GDP growth over time, a surprising pattern emerges: Economic growth does not reflect job growth. While India is abundant in unskilled and inexpensive labour, GDP growth has instead been powered by industries that prize skill and capital—scarce resources unavailable to a vast swathe of the country. The countless tales of success in the IT sector, automobile manufacturing, refined petrochemicals, telecommunications, and financial services are based on legitimate progress, but a progress that does not include much of India. It is not surprising then that the World Bank estimates that India needs to sustain GDP growth above 10 per cent every year for the next twenty years, just to maintain current levels of employment.[1]

The most curious part of this story is India's organized manufacturing sector. With its conveyor belts, repetitive tasks and predictability, manufacturing has, the world over, been seen as the poster child for an 'escalator' sector: It is more productive than agriculture, and has the potential to employ large numbers of workers, even if they have limited skills.

In India, however, the escalator from agriculture to manufacturing is stalled. Spurred by better access to capital, and coupled with the need to compete in increasingly integrated global markets, India's manufacturing industries have taken a route less dependent on labour. Construction has, in part, filled manufacturing's void by providing an immediate release valve for the workforce. This window will be open only temporarily, because incomes in agriculture and construction are converging. 'Retail trade'—the sector

The Curious Case of Indian Manufacturing—The Faster the Growth, the Fewer the Workers[2]

A Comparison of India's and Korea's Development Experience: Manufacturing Sub-sectors

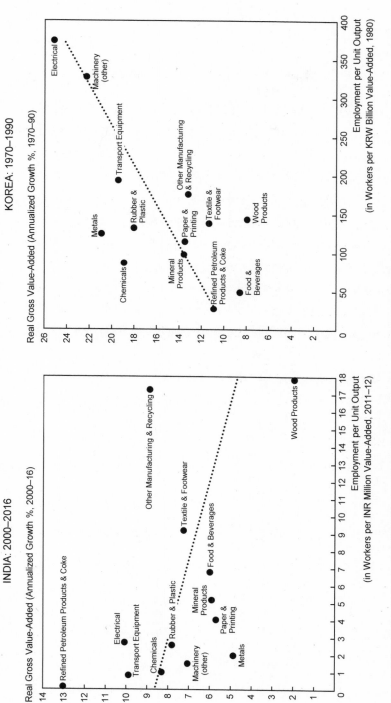

INDIA: 2000–2016

KOREA: 1970–1990

Source: Tata Sons Analysis; Reserve Bank of India KLEMS Data Release (2018); Korea Productivity Center KLEMS Database (2018)

that sells goods to people—has been the other outlet, and like construction, is overwhelmingly informal. It is dominated by small-scale, often part-time work, like selling vegetables from a cart, or household provisions from a shop.

The stalled escalator results in a situation where agriculture, which contributes 18 per cent to GDP, employs roughly 44 per cent of the workforce. Against this, the services sector contributes 52 per cent of GDP, but employs less than a third.[3]

India needs to create an environment for other sectors to flourish as escalators. Only then will workers step up from low-productivity industries to intermediate, and more productive work.

25

The Saju Mini Supermarket

The idea first came to Saju, Rajappa's younger son. Working after school hours at a local store, sorting plastic items for an extra buck, Saju picked up more than a pay cheque. He combed the neighbourhood for a viable business idea, anything that could keep his family afloat. He was all of eleven then, but intuitively it made sense to him—a vegetable stall wouldn't be tough to run.

Construction work had not put a dent in Rajappa's passion for farming. He liked the idea of selling vegetables— it seemed like a natural alternative to growing them. He hired a cart and tested the waters with a batch of leafy greens. But they sold less quickly than he had anticipated, and began to rot. Rajappa quickly changed track—vegetables with a longer shelf life made more sense. He woke up early to scour the markets for better potatoes, onions and tomatoes, to establish contacts with sellers, and to pursue business opportunities with bulk buyers.

Vegetables had not been Rajappa's first choice of business. He had tried selling colas and soft drinks, renting a small shop and investing in a refrigerator—the Saju Mini Supermarket was named after his youngest. That business had wrapped up quickly. They were in a poor neighbourhood, where everyone wanted things on credit. In no time, outstanding payments and receipts turned into a burden too heavy to bear. That was when Saju came up with the idea of the vegetable shop. Everybody was enthusiastic, but no one had anticipated how hard it would be.

The entire family chipped in—Saju before he left for school, Bijay between school and evening classes, Sangamma in the late afternoons, Bhoomi on the weekends, and Rajappa almost all of his waking hours when he wasn't buying vegetables or taking up waterproofing projects. He was so busy that he liked saying he couldn't afford friendship. The shop stayed open for over ten hours a day. They paid for the shop space, for transporting the vegetables, for the electricity, for the trade licence. To keep the rats at bay, the family even adopted a cat. But for all of this trouble, the Biyalis earned ₹500 ($7) a day at best, a sum Rajappa earned alone as a waterproofer on a decent day.

Only the promise of a regular income made running the shop worthwhile. It seemed to Rajappa, some days, that he was finally his own master, although Sangamma better saw the accounting: 'Owning a business' didn't really supplement Rajappa's earnings through construction work because now he rarely got any projects. With all their combined expenditure, Sangamma was certain they would not save a penny in this life.

Rajappa was proud of how well the children had fared at school, and insisted they study hard. But he wanted them to help out with the family business too. 'I feel they should spend half their time on studies and the rest on supplementing our incomes,' he said. 'We need them to help run the house and work to pay off our loans.' It made Sangamma uncomfortable. She wanted her children to escape this life. She wanted them to study. So what if they didn't save; they were investing in their future.

A few months after Bhoomi expressed doubts about her ability to continue with school, it became clear that Sangamma had prevailed over Rajappa, at least for the time being: Bhoomi returned to the eleventh grade for one more year of studies.

26

Investing in Fundamentals

Will India solve its jobs challenge by growing its way out of it? Probably not, given that economic growth does not translate to jobs in the same way as in the past.

Should India focus on sectors that have the potential to absorb large numbers of workers? (The debates in the front pages of India's newspapers, raging over exactly which sectors to pick, seem to suggest so.) This comes down to the nature of the jobs challenge. If people are unable to reach a basic standard of living because they want—but are out of—work, it makes sense to explore what activities will give rise to a greater number of jobs or provide more hours of work. In the case of India, this argument works for specific demographics that could be working, but are not: Women and youth, in particular. This is what the front-page debates miss—the arguments have merit, but these are not the target audiences that the headlining debates are always racing to solve for.

However, if large numbers of people are not reaching a minimum standard of living, despite working (and working hard), the country needs to look harder at productivity. This means looking at the quality of jobs, beyond looking at the quantum. This is the story of the Biyalis: They are a microcosm of the raw talent, industriousness and the motivation throughout the country, and their journey highlights some, but not all, of the realities of the transition from rural to urban, farm to non-farm. They embody India's jobs challenge.

Channelling the tremendous potential of the Biyalis throughout India requires not only more jobs, but better jobs. This means playing the right cards when it comes to both the strategic sectors that can drive employment as well as the nature and size of the country's firms.

A piece of the puzzle has been plainly in sight all along.

Everywhere Entrepreneurship

27

The Entrepreneur's Tale

A twenty-year-old Amit Singh, saw the value—the true value—of the college degree he was pursuing on the unforgettable day that he went out for a packet of biscuits. The owner of the kirana store recognized Amit's history textbooks, and mentioned that he had passed the same course a long time ago. The owner went on: Not only had he graduated, he had also topped his class. Amit looked at the man anew. He was surrounded by shelves full of biscuits, chips, breath mints, and matches in his tiny, ramshackle street-side stall. All Amit could say was, 'Then how did you end up here?'[1]

The store owner explained. On graduating, he had unsuccessfully applied for a series of Rajasthan government jobs, then failed to find work as a teacher, couldn't become a railway officer, and someone else always got the bank peon jobs. At each turn, there were far more qualified, and even overqualified, candidates than positions available. After several attempts, he gave up all dreams of finding a stable job. There were always more newspaper announcements to answer, more forms to fill, and more qualifying exams to give. But why would anyone put themselves through all that? He decided to start this store out of sheer necessity.[2]

As the storekeeper relived his past, Amit saw his own future.

Amit is in his late thirties now. He smiled as he remembered what happened next, all those years ago. It was a long story, but one he enjoyed telling.

The meeting with the man had shaken him. But just weeks later, he chanced upon a brochure for a textile manufacturing course at an apparel training institute in Jaipur, just 150 kilometres away from Alwar where he was pursuing his Bachelor of Arts in History. Jaipur was famous for the clothes it exported. He wanted to be there.

First, though, he had to arrange an amount three times his family's monthly earnings for the course. 'I never felt awkward about not having money,' he said. Prices weren't set in stone. He asked the training institute's principal for a discount, and got away with paying half. 'If you don't reach out for what you need,' Amit said, 'you lose out in life.'

Discounts on rent, meals and travel were harder to come by. For a long time, he struggled to pay. Then, wandering through a trade show in Delhi, he found a company selling embroidery and screen-printing machines, which he knew nothing about. He cornered the company's owners and asked them everything. What made the embroidery multi-coloured? How did it organize threads by number and colour? Did a long stitch take as long to administer as a short one? This is an entrepreneur's story, so what follows is predictable: They hired him as an intern there and then.

Amit's duties at the factory began at eight in the evening and ended at two in the morning, while he attended the manufacturing course during the day. He slept on the factory floor near the embroidery machines. He could finally meet the costs of living, but he loved it for a different reason: He was receiving an education that no training institute could provide.

28

The End of the Shift

The apparel training institute that Amit attended struggled to set up learning opportunities for students. If a factory visit opened up, the institute told students to 'arrive at the factory on time, stand in line, ask no questions, inconvenience no one, hurry along, and return home,' Amit recalled. During one of these visits, Amit, along with the other students, was kept waiting at the gate for hours and then told that the visit was cancelled because buyers were visiting the factory that day.

Amit decided to scout for an opportunity himself. He made his way to another manufacturing house where he talked to the general manager about shop floor efficiency techniques. The manager told him to calculate how much time each of the 500 tailors on the shop floor took to stitch a shirt using a particular technique. Tailors are categorized by their speed, and paid accordingly. Amit's calculations showed that most of them were slower than their categories suggested, and that the factory could save 10 per cent every month by optimizing the categories. The manager offered him a job.

Amit hadn't had time to study for the institute's tests, but when he was asked to list three measurements for a shirt, he recited forty. The examiner demanded to know where he had copied his answers from, he recalled.

Overall, Amit found the course dissatisfying, and focused more on his work at the factory. Meanwhile, his parents began to look for a wife for him. They imagined someone who could offer a double bed and a fridge, perhaps even a car, as dowry. But Amit, who had been impressed by the doctor-dentist couples who ran clinics together, wanted a partner with an entrepreneurial bent. When Niyati—whose parents kept pressing her to marry, even though she wanted to be a fashion designer in Jaipur—came up as a prospect, Amit reasoned that at least she was from his line of work.

They married, and soon after he wanted to quit work to start a business with her. Niyati advised caution; she had seen her parents' home grow from one room to three over several years. It was all because of the stability their jobs provided. 'You cannot spring up a staircase in one bound. You have to do it step by step. And don't forget that people like us don't have a lift,' she told him.

He listened. He sourced merchandise, he checked for defects, he waited for the right moment. When someone offered him a million rupees ($14,000) to approve a consignment of defective clothes, he refused. Trust was the currency in the future he had envisioned.

Waiting is hard, though. For reassurance, Niyati and Amit solicited a seer's advice, but came away grumbling about a bleak prediction—the seer had announced that Amit would fail in the garments business.

It was five years since their marriage. They had a daughter. The year was 2014, and there was optimism and talk of change in the air. It felt like the right moment had arrived. Just to be safe, they named the business after their daughter Shreya—one of many names for the Hindu goddess of wealth.

29

The Great Skew

India famously has large business houses like the Tatas with thousands, even hundreds of thousands, of employees. At the other end are tiny firms that hire fewer than ten workers. Between them is a vast emptiness where dynamic companies that are neither gargantuan nor minuscule should be. The official shorthand for these companies is 'Small and Medium Enterprises' (SMEs). These firms could provide the bulk of productive employment in India if they existed in larger numbers. But they don't. We think of this space as India's engine for creating more and better jobs—a productive alternative to the informal sector, for the millions of people leaving agriculture as well as those who are entering the workforce in the coming decade.[1]

To understand India's skewed employment profile, consider this: The average firm in India employs just over two people. This is because the bulk of private sector workers—about 70 per cent—work in micro firms, while just over 10 per cent are employed by SMEs. In the United States, SMEs account for 36 per cent of private sector employment. In Germany, they employ 43 per cent. In Brazil, 39 per cent.[2]

Comparisons only prove how unusual India's case is. The textile and apparel sector that Amit is a part of is one of the largest employers in India, after agriculture and construction. In the Chinese apparel sector, employment in firms with fewer than eight workers makes up less than 5 per cent of total employment. For India, the corresponding figure is over 80 per cent.[3]

Micro enterprises are often informal, with low productivity and few prospects for growth. They have little ability to invest in machinery and equipment for their businesses. For their owners, rewards are scant; for employees, they barely provide a livelihood. Not large enough to enjoy economies of scale, and lacking exposure to modern processes and techniques, they remain small— never realizing the improvements in productivity that go hand-in-hand with growth and formalization. The foregone productivity is substantial; an Indian manufacturing firm of 50–200 employees is nearly four times as productive as one with between five and fifty. The differences between the formal and informal sector are even more stark. Formal sector manufacturing firms are eight times as productive.[4]

Micro Firms Dominate India's Employment Landscape, Unlike Its Global Peers[5]

Distribution of Employment by Firm Size

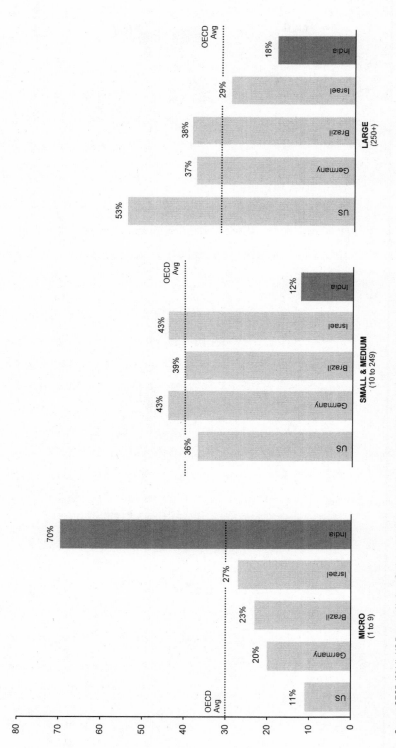

Private Sector Employment (%)

Source: OECD (2014); US Bureau of Labour Statistics (2014); Economic Census of India (2014); and Tata Sons–Dalberg analysis

Most micro enterprises are simply self-employed individuals running their own businesses—say, a paan or a kirana shop. They are entrepreneurs largely because they have been unable to find salaried jobs. These 'enterprises' make up more than 70 per cent of India's firms.[6]

This isn't the typical image that comes to mind when people think of entrepreneurship. They imagine 'unicorns'—high-growth, venture-funded tech start-ups valued at over a billion dollars that attract the headlines. India currently has eighteen of these. It is possible that they could one day employ—directly or indirectly—thousands or even millions of people. But India needs jobs in the tens of millions. In 2018, for instance, tech start-ups employed about 170,000 people directly, and created employment for 500,000 indirectly, hiring around 40,000 new workers in the year. These are all big numbers, but in India, there's always a bigger number. Micro firms employed nearly 121 million people in 2014. The cumulative effect of hundreds of thousands of SMEs could be massive.[7]

30

Goldilocks Entrepreneurs

Amit understood needles and stitches, time-and-motion studies and manufacturing crises. He did not yet understand the other things that entrepreneurs faced: the trouble in getting basic services, in getting electricity, in getting a loan, in finding land. While seeking a loan, he found himself spending days in the branch of a large public sector bank, wrestling with paperwork and trying to convince the bank officers of the viability of his business. After missing ten days of work, and still facing additional demands for changes and information, Amit gave up on the attempt entirely.

As of 2017, the total supply of credit to SMEs and micro enterprises was estimated to be around ₹70 trillion ($1 trillion). About 84 per cent of this came from informal sources, including self-financing, loans from friends and family, and moneylenders. The rest was from banks, non-banking financial companies, government financial institutions, and other formal sources. Public sector banks, which provided ₹5.4 trillion ($77 billion)—nearly half of all formal credit—to these enterprises, found that 12 per cent of their loans were non-performing assets and likely had to be written down. This, unsurprisingly, has led to caution.[1]

Amit had given private banks a try previously. He recalled an interview with an agent for a ₹1 million loan ($14,000). At the time, he was running a factory out of a temporary shed near an industrial area. The interview, which took place at Amit's factory, seemed designed to browbeat him. The agent was clearly unimpressed with what he saw. His questions betrayed his suspicions. 'What will you do if your business suffers a loss? What collateral do you have to repay the loan? What if you get kicked off the property? What if you cannot repay the loan and are destitute?'

After a certain point, Amit found the questions insulting. 'What if you meet with an accident going home? How will you file your report then?' he snapped back at the agent. The man was not amused. Amit's loan request was turned down. The agent's boss then called to say that while Amit's report was not promising, they could have a meeting to 'settle' the matter. There was always some problem or the other with banks. It became clear they would only lend Amit money if he could prove he had a permanent establishment—the very thing Amit was seeking a loan to build.

He didn't even know of the existence of credit from small, regional and local banks, that are often tasked with filling the credit gap for entrepreneurs like him. In Europe and the United States for instance, they provide loans to a third of all SMEs. This figure is only 6 per cent in India. Their branches make up only 15 per cent of all bank branches in India, in contrast to 32 per cent in Europe.[2]

Amit's faith in government policies and incentives was quickly dashed too. Nothing he found applied to someone starting off at his level. If anything, he realized, popular government schemes tended to encourage and further the growth of businesses that were already established, or else catered to micro entrepreneurs.

He was too small for some and yet, not small enough for others—a Goldilocks entrepreneur.

He could not, for instance, get a traditional business loan because he had nothing to offer by way of collateral. His firm was too large to access micro enterprise schemes like MUDRA loans or microfinance. Amit would almost definitely not be on the radar of a venture capitalist because of his inability to scale rapidly and the limited innovation in his business model.[3]

'Small businesses have a 100 per cent risk and attract 0 per cent sympathy,' Amit said. 'A big businessman gets 30- and 50-days credit from his suppliers, but if I ask for the same credit, they say no.'

Even specially demarcated commercial land meant to facilitate trade just ended up in the hands of more powerful people. As a small businessman, Amit could barely make rent. He tried to get an electrical connection for small industries that assured him of power at a lower tariff, but the experience was so onerous that he settled instead for regular power.

Amit remembered the struggle. 'When I asked an exporter how to do business, he said, "This is bad work, full of losses." People are insecure that you will take their work.' Amit soldiered on, renting a tin shed in a slum so that he could undercut rivals, commuting on a bike, juggling three jobs. There were times he wanted to give it all up. 'I thought of leaving the stitching business, but my wife insisted I continue.'

Step by step, just as his wife had said, they found ways forward. They ate cheaply if they went out, holidays were spent at home, and cash gifts from relatives were saved. They needed the money to buy land, build a factory, pay for materials, and buy machines. It wasn't like someone would just give them the capital they needed.

So, imagine his surprise when an exporter who trusted him gave him the land for a factory for a small down payment. 'We'll figure out the rest,' he remembered the exporter saying, appreciating that someone believed in him.

Amit didn't think his struggles were over. Even today, with fifty machines on hand, and a turnover of ₹25 million

($350,000) a year, he doubted anyone would extend him a business loan. Still, if there was one person he could rely on, it was his indomitable self. 'I always felt like if others can do it, why not me?'

•—•

In recent years, Amit found that formalization came with its own costs. He hired a full-time accountant for ₹25,000 ($350) a month to keep records straight and navigate the new Goods and Services Tax (GST) filing system, which he found complicated. 'I don't mind paying taxes, but the processes are too extensive. I used to manage this before myself, but now to tally things is impossible.' He added, 'At least everything is digital and above board, and there are no unpleasant surprises later.'[4]

Amit was less sanguine about paying an agency to keep abreast of labour laws and regulations, which numbered over 200 across state and central levels, with over 1,800 possible filings annually for larger firms. 'The formalities involved are too complex for a business person to manage,' he said. 'You need to meticulously detail your submissions by number of employees, hours worked, daily wages of so much, and you need to format it accordingly.' Any deviance would attract a notice from the Ministry of Labour and then it would be a 'tension waali baat', a stressful matter.[5]

In the last few years, India has shot up fifty-three places in the Ease of Doing Business rankings, which assesses countries on ten different dimensions including credit, property, registration and taxes. This has not necessarily translated to an easier business environment for small and medium entrepreneurs like Amit.[6]

The average number of days to register commercial property in more developed states (such as Maharashtra, Gujarat and Delhi) is 116 days. In Uttar Pradesh, Chhattisgarh and Odisha, the time taken is higher—136 days on average. These two figures are far higher than the time used in the official rankings, based on Mumbai (eighty-five days) and Delhi (fifty-five days). Against this, the average in high-income OECD countries is only twenty days.[7]

There is one part of the ease of doing business that all states and cities perform poorly in: Enforcing contracts and efficiency of the judicial system. In this category, India is still ranked 163rd out of 190 countries. Even in Mumbai and Delhi, the time it takes to resolve a contract dispute through the judicial process is 1,445 days versus 582 days in high-income OECD countries. Entrepreneurs feel the weight of slow dispute resolution. Small business owners naturally struggle to absorb the high costs and loss of revenue caused by lengthy judicial proceedings.[8]

•—•

India's focus on the two extremes of entrepreneurship—high-growth start-ups and micro enterprises—has inevitably meant a lack of focus on entrepreneurs like Amit. It is in between these two extremes that the country will need to invest. India needs many SMEs, each of whom may not individually hire many people, but collectively, they can provide a quantum of productive employment that the country needs. And they need to be spread across the country—not just in the major economic centres. Since these types of firms use local inputs and often start off by catering to local demand, they can be drivers of widespread development, drawing the informal and formal sectors closer together.

We call this the 'everywhere entrepreneurship' movement. The bright lights of this movement are local SMEs—the restaurant, health clinic, salon, textile manufacturer and car garage—that use tried and tested business models to solve local problems. They are unlikely to become tomorrow's large corporations, but stitched together, they are integral to the future of India.

31

A Solitary Enterprise

Facing these challenges can be a solitary endeavour for business owners like Amit. True to his dream, however, he has an equal partner in Niyati, and this lightens the otherwise lonely weight of being an entrepreneur. Niyati now maintains their long-standing relationship with Japanese customers and comes up with new designs that can be easily produced in India and which match their tastes and market appetites. She undertakes the negotiations and oversees the production of these garments until they are shipped.

When asked who his business role models were, Amit could not recall anyone from his district who had success as an entrepreneur. Garments exports did not even exist as an activity there, when he started off. The region had changed in the last decade, with newer factory and industrial areas popping up, and improved road and train connectivity. But the old ways of thinking hadn't changed, he said. 'In my village, shop owners, brick layers, builders—they have all inherited their parents' profession. Practically everyone in my village works for ₹10,000–15,000 ($140–210) per month and that is considered a stable life. I tried encouraging my own nephew with offers of financial assistance and mentoring, but he doesn't want to take a risk and start a business.'

In the United States, Amit's story would have been the very embodiment of 'the American Dream'. In India, his story was not perceived as one of success but as one of a failure to get a job. It didn't seem to matter that his apparel-manufacturing unit was a multi-storey building, employed fifty people, and had orders from across Asia and Europe.

Niyati explained, 'Even today our relatives say, "Oh good, you are managing, but how far will you go before it all comes down? You do not even have a son to inherit this. Better to have stuck to your job, at least you would have the leisure to enjoy your life on weekends."' She added, in a sombre tone, 'Business involves you bowing down to circumstances and people in order to come out on top. It is not something our family members find palatable.'

Big production units often make Amit tempting offers—a fancier house, a faster car and a stable job. But what they offer pales in comparison to the pride he felt the day his daughter distributed Diwali laddoos to his community of 200-odd well-wishers, dyers, embroiderers, traders, suppliers, buyers and employees.

The level of grit, determination and occasional luck that is present throughout Amit's story shows why people like Amit who find success as entrepreneurs are rare. Encouraging everywhere entrepreneurship would mean allowing more people to be successful without requiring the heroic levels of resourcefulness and courage that Amit and Niyati were forced to muster.

If India is to become a nation where the Amits of the world can thrive, it will need a fundamental shift in how it supports and nurtures entrepreneurship. Amit describes his experience best when he says, 'I wasn't given wings to fly, so I had to keep inching forward.'

32

Embracing Everywhere
Entrepreneurship

Today, not enough people choose to become entrepreneurs—
they are forced into it. Those who do, find that success is
hard to come by. They lack access to the credit, markets,
skilled labour and infrastructure necessary to expand their
business, and hire more people. Compound all this with
stubborn red tape, and it becomes easier to understand why
entrepreneurs like Amit are rare in India.

Making India a hub of everywhere entrepreneurs will be
no easy task. It will require reforming institutions with the
power to shape markets, and changing widespread attitudes
about entrepreneurship, by making it something to aspire to.

Other countries have walked this path before. South
Korea and Singapore, for instance, adopted national industrial
policies that focused on building a base of entrepreneurs.
Rwanda adopted a national strategy that explicitly linked

a sense of patriotism with an entrepreneurial spirit, using everything from national media campaigns to a mandatory entrepreneurship curriculum.[1]

It's clear that a combination of education and exposure improves a country's awareness and acceptance of entrepreneurship as a viable career path. For countries like India, the impact can be outsized. Research shows that the lower the starting point, the greater the effect education can have on a country's 'culture' of entrepreneurship.[2]

The goal of an entrepreneurship education isn't simply to make it more appealing, but to change the way students think. The right curriculum can improve non-academic skills such as creativity, persistence, teamwork, and can encourage comfort with risk-taking. These skills are crucial to success in a future of work that is likely to be deeply entrepreneurial in spirit. Arguably, they are also integral to citizenship and nation-building.

WHAT COULD ENTREPRENEURSHIP EDUCATION IN INDIA LOOK LIKE?

Entrepreneurship education is different from core school subjects which are traditionally teacher-led, and tested with exams. With entrepreneurship education, the focus is not as much on learning concepts as it is about building skills, such as the ability to collaborate and communicate. These skills cannot be taught and tested like core subjects, but can be developed through a learning-by-doing approach. The cultural mindset of students will have to be considered, and approaches need to be tailored by state.

States like Delhi and Bihar are already experimenting with different approaches. In Bihar, for instance, 'Going To School', an NGO, is enabling government-run schools to deliver entrepreneurship education through stories, games and projects. The focus is to enable students to learn problem-solving by creating business plans. The impact of entrepreneurship education has been tangible. Grade 9 students believe that an entrepreneur is someone 'who is fearless and is able to face any outcome'. A study revealed improvements of up to 6 per cent per year on the entrepreneurial skills children learned—creative problem solving, understanding business, and networking and collaboration.

With education must come other structural changes over the long term. The roads that transport goods must be better, and the electricity needed to produce them must be easier to acquire. Much has been said about the shifts in policy necessary for credit access, labour, and regulatory oversight.

The scale of the challenge regulations create for businesses is sometimes glossed over. Labour regulations in

India have seventeen definitions of 'workers' and twenty-two definitions of 'wages'. More than forty laws regulate labour—the condition of hiring and termination, wages, workplace safety and so on—at just the national level; several states have modified or introduced additional laws of their own. Each law, each regulation, comes with its own documentation requirements, inspections, clearances and penalties.[3]

Whatever reform path India decides to take, SMEs should find a place at the centre of new policy design. India is all too familiar with well-intentioned policies that have unintended consequences. For example, existing labour policy mandates a series of deductions from a formal employees' gross salary, to ensure enough savings for retirement. The policy is well-meaning. However, the trade-offs are substantial in the arithmetic of lower-income workers, who may often need to forgo long-term savings in order to deal with immediate, daily expenses. They can view the potential 20 to 30 per cent difference between what they cost to a firm and what they get to take home, as a luxury they cannot afford—this becomes an incentive to work informally and negotiate the value of the monthly contributions as extra cash-in-hand. In effect, the structure ends up being a tax on formal employment.[4]

From where SMEs stand, these are the sort of laws and regulations that need the most urgent reform—the ones that stifle growth at the low end, making demands that few entrepreneurs are capable of meeting.

Capturing India's entrepreneurial spirit means a transformation of vision away from a culture of micro-management. The fact is that the country must embrace SME growth. Growth will come not from pushing hard, but from removing the obstacles SMEs face. Each hurdle would be problematic on its own, but together they turn basic economic activities into Herculean tasks that erode confidence and lead to a vicious cycle of low-trust interactions. These numerous obstacles can tilt the scales on whether it is worthwhile to start or grow a business.

A certain level of judicious risk-taking accompanies this growth mindset. In response, SMEs require supervision, not suspicion. Smart risk management doesn't force more control, more rules and more policies but improves oversight of existing rules, while simplifying them.

This is the long-term vision that needs to take hold. To get started right away, we believe a technology-led approach can dismantle some of the obstacles SMEs face.

Bengalurus Everywhere

Compared with entrepreneurs across India, Bengaluru's start-ups have it made. There's finance available for every stage of a company's lifecycle, specialized services for marketing and IT support, distributor networks, and a galaxy of mentors, advisors, peers and competitors. Even clients are only a traffic jam away.

The barriers that keep would-be entrepreneurs elsewhere in India from starting up have successfully been dismantled—or at least substantially lowered—in Bengaluru. Of course, this is true only for a certain kind of person: The typical start-up founder in Bengaluru tends to be from India's more privileged classes, and enjoys significant social capital and financial security. They are also likely to have relevant industry exposure, and have the financial buffers to stick with a start-up idea even if it takes a while to succeed.

What is it about Bengaluru that enables entrepreneurs to thrive? And how can India replicate those lessons? The challenge is to provide a Bengaluru-like support system to someone who has nothing in common with the typical tech start-up founder—a person much like Amit.

Start-up Entrepreneurs in Bengaluru Can Access a Range of Business Services

Source: Tata Sons analysis

198

Governments have attempted to boost clusters of SMEs by creating special economic zones where land acquisition is simplified, and companies can enjoy tax breaks. However, these zones are not a substitute for an ecosystem, and have rarely ended up creating many SMEs.[5]

We believe that a cluster should be shaped by local context—natural endowments like proximity to a port, a transport hub or a specific natural resource; as well as social endowments like universities that create a pool of skilled human capital. Various parts of the country already have advantages and resources of their own. By building a community of practitioners and institutions, we can enable everywhere entrepreneurs, already familiar with the local context, to take advantage of opportunities to create firms. What would such a cluster look like?

Bridgital Clusters Can Spur Everywhere Entrepreneurship

There are 722 districts in India. To create a physical cluster in each of them would be daunting. But the range of services and practices that form the core of an effective cluster can be made available to them if we move beyond a physical-only mindset. Digital technologies provide the opportunity to extend Bengaluru-like services to local businesses across the country.[6]

Take finance: Digital lending companies are using cashflow history, psychometric assessments and social media behaviour to assess lending risks. An everywhere entrepreneur could potentially use such platforms to access credit without a standard credit score or collateral, irrespective of whether they live in a city or a village. Digital recruitment and training are also becoming mainstream. An everywhere entrepreneur who needs to hire a skilled worker no longer has to approach a labour agency to find workers.

Creating a Bridgital cluster will need a crucial piece of innovation—a 'platform of platforms' that provides entrepreneurs with an easy way to access services. A functional platform could help the proliferation of everywhere entrepreneurs wherever they are based in India. The greatest value of a Bridgital cluster is that it democratizes a range of services that only formal businesses can access today. This has the potential to make the everywhere entrepreneurship movement truly inclusive, involving even small, informal entrepreneurs.

Entrepreneurs themselves may be hesitant to sign on to such services. When we told Amit about platforms that provide unsecured digital lending, he was sceptical. He was worried about getting scammed, in part because his last experience with e-commerce went poorly.[7] Added to this, even though he engaged with banks personally and offered collateral, Amit could not get a business loan. He found it hard to believe that a stranger who had never met him was willing to approve a loan without collateral. As Amit (and others) grow more comfortable with digital finance, they will perhaps be willing to try applying for loans online as well. Until then, even if they do nothing else, they are still building a crucial data trail.

For an entrepreneur looking at all the features of a formal firm today, the list of tasks is daunting. There are accounts to look after, contracts and benefits for workers, a payroll and leave system, tax filings. It is as if someone standing at the foot of a cliff were asked to bound straight to the top, in a single leap: Perhaps they could indeed attain that height, but it's impractical to expect it all in one step.

The creation of a Bridgital cluster changes the landscape: it breaks down those various services into discrete modules, each representing a small step that a business could take, if it saw value in doing so. Each step takes the business a little closer to the formal end of the spectrum. In this process, Bridgital clusters can be enablers of trust, by providing verified digital services. Firms can be freed to forge their own paths to formality.

The High Costs of Formality Will Be Lowered in a Bridgital World[8]

An Illustration of the Steps to Formality for Businesses

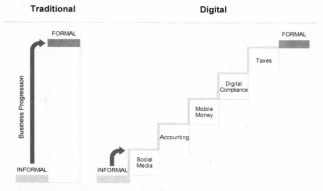

Source: Center for Global Development; Tata Sons analysis

This is why boosting the use of digital technology should be one of India's paramount priorities. The fact is that 68 per cent of SMEs are 'offline'—they have never used an Internet connection for any business purpose, or might not even have one. Deliberately pushing digital adoption can, we believe, provide a quantum leap to the MSME sector and bring firms increasingly into the digital and formal fold.[9]

Digital Governance: Simplicity and Scale

No amount of digital innovation will help if SMEs' biggest hurdle isn't resolved—dealing with government regulations and the bureaucracy. For one, compliance with existing policies can be and should be made easier. Digitizing government services is a powerful way to simplify processes.

Among other things, e-governance systems significantly reduce the instance of cumbersome paperwork; if combined with rules that set time limits on the processing of applications, it can bring a measure of certainty as well.

Take enterprise registration. Until recently, the registration process for SMEs varied by states and methods (digital or manual). But after 2015, all SME registrations require signing a single-page form. The form can be completed online, and the entrepreneur is only required to self-certify their details. Similarly, the Ministry of Labour and Employment has put together an online portal as a single point of contact for employer, employee and enforcement agencies to increase transparency and accountability in labour inspection. More digitization of this kind can save entrepreneurs' time, energy and paperwork.

An approach that sees different government departments independently undertaking digitization initiatives, however, will not be enough. SMEs have to deal with multiple levels and different divisions of the bureaucracy. Manufacturing SMEs, for instance, have to provide the same set of documents—factory architecture layouts, lease deeds, registration information and electricity bills—to the municipality for, say, a fire safety certification, and to the state government for a pollution control certification. Speak to any entrepreneur for long enough and similar stories come pouring out. For some, compliance is a sinkhole of valuable time; for others, not having the right piece of paper means an opportunity missed.

Digital Governance Can Transform the Relationship between SMEs and the Bureaucracy[10]

An Illustrative Example of the 'Once Only Principle' in E-Governance Systems

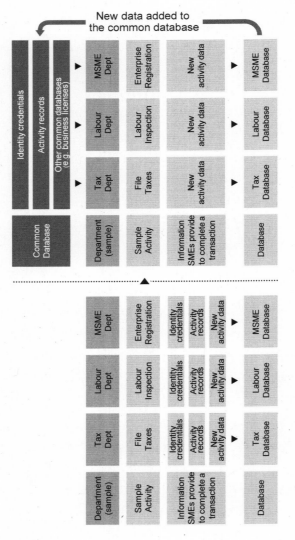

Source: Policy Options Politiques; Tata Sons analysis

As SMEs drive economic and employment growth, their challenges will grow more complex. The real imperative is to eschew piecemeal digitization, attempting instead to transform the relationship between SMEs and the government. It is not only about limiting the duplication of effort for entrepreneurs, but also bringing growth opportunities—many may be unaware of government incentives and export schemes they qualify for—to their doorstep. This will need the adoption of best-practice e-governance systems and principles.

Estonia, one of the early adopters of e-governance, follows a 'once only principle' for data collection to streamline interactions with the bureaucracy. Citizens and businesses provide their information to the government only once. Thereafter, this information is available to every government department. Estonia's digital governance is estimated to save more than 800 years of working time for the state and citizens every year. A similar approach could greatly benefit India's SMEs, and the ease of doing business more broadly.[11]

India may be a thousand times the size of Estonia, but as we point out throughout this book—the beauty of a digital approach is that scale can take hold.

33

Small Business, Large Impact

Janvi, a classmate of Bhoomi's, used to dream of becoming a cardiologist. 'Now, I want to start a company that makes the machines that will perform cardiac surgeries,' she said.

That moment spoke volumes. India needs to find ways to keep pace with the Amits, while anticipating the Janvis throughout the country. They can be the employers of the future for millions.

For a sense of how different India would look with everywhere entrepreneurship, consider the following illustration. If SMEs' share of employment looked closer to that of India's peers—say, at 30 per cent by 2030—India would have eight million SMEs, generating more productive employment for about 80 million workers. Compared to baseline projections, this amounts to an increase of about five million SMEs and 45 million jobs in more formal and productive firms.[1]

Everywhere Entrepreneurship Could Lift 45 Million Indians into Productive Employment

Distribution of India's Workforce (Current and Potential) with Everywhere Entrepreneurship

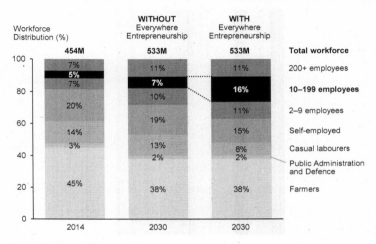

Source: Tata Sons and Dalberg analysis

The power of everywhere entrepreneurship is that it is possible for these types of entrepreneurs to exist in every community around the country. They can help meet local needs and develop local resources, spurring development in the communities where they operate. Because they can be ubiquitous, they can—in the aggregate—produce far more employment than the small size of any individual firm might suggest. These everywhere entrepreneurs are also more likely to expand their businesses and make the investments in technology that improve the productivity of their firms and workers.

•—•

The twin challenges you have been reading about in these chapters—jobs and access—call for a plan for the twenty-first century that Indians can get behind. Fundamentally, this plan should renew the focus on entrepreneurship to move the needle towards formal employers; it should make paid work attractive for women in order to address the participation gap; and ultimately, this plan will need to be anchored by a Bridgital approach that marries the gap between skills and jobs.

Done with purpose and urgency, India can transform the lives of hundreds of millions, unleash huge productivity gains in concert, and tap into vast reserves of undiscovered economic fuel. The gains of the Bridgital approach aren't theoretical. A taste of this promising future exists today, beyond the rocky hills 60 kilometres east of Bengaluru, near the gold fields of Kolar.

Bridgital in Action

34

New Aims

On visiting the All India Institute of Medical Sciences (AIIMS) in New Delhi in 2016, K.R. Ramesh Kumar, then the health minister of Karnataka, had braced himself for disorder. This was where the country's finest doctors gathered to be pressure-cooked by the nine thousand patients who arrived at the hospital's forty-eight outpatient departments every day. Hundreds would wait hopefully for an elusive appointment slot, visiting multiple times a day or over weeks until they got one. Patients lay on beds anywhere and everywhere. Everybody had questions, and nobody had answers.

But the minister was befuddled. There were queues and quiet. There were electronic displays, token numbers and tablets. Things moved quickly.

The orderliness was by design. The AIIMS Transformation project was a venture by TCS to streamline patient movement through the hospital. The average waiting time after getting an appointment fell from six hours to two. Four in five patients arrived with appointments, up from one in five. There was a new class of workers he hadn't seen before—they coordinated between doctors and patients. The adjustments and larger changes made to achieve such a system were many, but at its heart was a simple offering: Clear information for doctors and patients alike. It hadn't required a miracle, or vast investments in building something new and untested. The system used what was already available. Just differently.

Minister Kumar wanted to transform healthcare in Karnataka. He knew that out in the countryside, where most of India lived, healthcare needed some kind of order. He knew, all too well, that patients ignored the primary health centres made for them and headed straight to hospitals. He wanted to give them something better.

In August 2017, Minister Kumar met with the Tata Group to build on the system he had seen at AIIMS. Only this would not be confined to a building, but spread over an entire district in Karnataka. They would begin in his constituency, the rocky outpost named Kolar.

•—•

Kolar is neither rich nor poor. Its income level is close to the national median. Its literacy rate is only marginally lower than the rest of Karnataka, but it has more children who drop out of school. Once known for its gold fields, Kolar is now famous for its tomatoes. It is not uncommon, in certain years, to see farmers destroying unwanted tomatoes by leaving them on the highway and letting passing cars do the rest.[1]

The town bustles with markets and traffic, but at the edges, it thins and turns quiet. Roads become single lanes on the town's outskirts. Among the hills that resemble giant rock piles, there are even narrower paths of mud to villages hidden somewhere in the distance. Bus stops are remote, and simply reaching them means walking a long stretch, or taking a ride over bumpy terrain. For people who sit in wait in the tree shade to hail a ride or catch sight of a bus, crossing these distances is a decision measured in money and time. If their destination is the district hospital in Kolar, their calculations include the possibility of malfunctioning machines and missing doctors. A day gone to waste.

The future of Kolar's healthcare, it was decided, would begin at one edge of the town, in a sanatorium where langurs and wild horses strolled through the corridors. An unused room was set aside for the system, which by now had a name—Digital Nerve Centre, or DiNC.

The DiNC model worked in two ways, just as the AIIMS transformation did. By redefining certain roles and responsibilities, and creating a new class of Bridgital workers, time-consuming administrative pressures were taken off valuable medical staff. And with the added mesh of technology, the system sorted patients at the very beginning, and brought more people into healthcare's purview.

The team from TCS that built the system for AIIMS knew about healthcare systems and processes. They were dealing with practices that had calcified so long ago that few understood how strange things had become.

When the team looked at how specialist doctors— oncological surgeons, to be precise—spent their days, it came as a surprise to know that only around half their time was spent treating people. The rest of it involved non-clinical work: Filing paperwork, developing checklists, writing notes for the operation theatre, and explaining the modalities of diagnostic tests to patients. It was work someone else could be doing. Even clinical time often included patients with basic ailments who would have been better served if they had visited a primary or secondary health facility.

In simpler terms, doctors' capacity was severely hamstrung. They found that when just one of their tasks— operation theatre notes—was shifted, it created enough time for them to see more patients. On just this one task among the dozens that India's oncologists performed every day, the shift translated to nearly 4,000 extra doctor-hours every year.[2] Numbers were on their side. Given India's size, the slightest improvement would make a huge difference.

The TCS team had reimagined the processes of India's largest public hospital, and created a national network that linked cancer hospitals. But the task of helping supplement primary healthcare meant dealing with public infrastructure, organizing government doctors and nurses, and reordering entrenched processes. Unexpected surprises were inevitable.

They didn't have to wait long. While the rest of the sanatorium had electricity, it took two months for DiNC to finally have access to the power they required. In the meantime, in the western extension of the building, they began to arrange clusters of desks where nurses and doctors would sit, making phones calls, receiving questions. Unlike call centres aimed outside India's borders, this centre's focus would be deeply local. The team's members began to train local recruits in the art of primary healthcare outreach.

There was no better way to do this than to enlist community health workers, one of India's great public health successes.

35

ASHAs

'What, Ammi, still doing homework at this age? When will you stop?'

Aminah Sheikh grinned at her thirteen-year-old son and kept working. She hadn't yet changed out of her pink saree, the uniform that told people from a distance that she was a health worker. As always, it was lined with dust from the day's exertions: Walking from hut to hut, asking questions, offering guidance, taking notes. She sat on the floor of her own hut and prepared a report about the house visits on her tablet. The connection kept breaking, and she stepped out to wave the tablet in the darkness until it caught a signal.

Aminah had turned thirty in the past year. She raised her children alone in Juhalli, a village in Kolar. She had studied until seventh grade, was married by sixteen, and divorced at twenty. She took on tailoring jobs for a living, but gave it up because 'everyone in the village knows how to sew. Everyone makes their own clothes at home.' Ten years ago, she signed up to become an ASHA during a recruitment drive.[1] There was no salary, but there was an honorarium, and there were commissions for every child they got immunized, and every new and expectant mother they sent to a doctor or followed up on.

She had met Geetha, a fellow ASHA, then, and they had been inseparable ever since. Between them, they covered Kannada and Urdu, the languages of the villages they had been assigned. All the better to tell off the drunk and belligerent men they encountered on occasion. 'Having someone else with you is better in such cases. You don't feel unsafe,' Aminah said. Once out in the field, they accompanied pregnant women for delivery, ensured that babies were immunized, checked up on antenatal and prenatal cases, and distributed medicines to tuberculosis patients.

Lately, their roles had been expanded as part of a new project. They had recently been trained to screen people for non-communicable diseases that included diabetes, heart disease and cancer. They were also paid to register people on the healthcare system their tablets were connected with. Each new registration earned them a rupee over the monthly ₹3,500 ($50) they now earned. The tablet in their hand had made access into households easier, Aminah said. 'It makes people curious. They have not seen something like this before. They think it is a big deal having their details on this device. So, now they flock to us with their Aadhaar cards to get registered.'

The tablets were an extension of DiNC's efforts to enrol residents across Kolar. ASHAs were among the first to experience the change. 'There are some things that are different now, which we like,' Geetha said. Aminah agreed. (They usually agreed with each other.) 'Earlier, we would have to wait for a weekly visit from a nurse to the primary health centre for screenings. We didn't have any means of helping people get appointments at the hospital. Now, we do this screening ourselves and people think well of us because we can establish contact with the hospital.'

'I think,' Aminah said, 'our status in society has improved.'

36

The Clinicograph

After the introduction of ASHAs nearly a decade and a half ago, India's maternal and child health parameters improved dramatically. ASHAs came from the community they worked in, spoke the language, and knew its concerns. They encouraged expectant mothers to visit doctors, and kept following up.

ASHAs were also tasked with gathering data. But the records they maintained were on paper, with all the difficulties the medium possessed. Information was updated irregularly and difficult to audit. With the government's approval, TCS team members taught ASHAs to register new patients on tablets, ask questions that could identify undiagnosed illnesses, and record data about the people they met almost instantly. ASHAs would lead the charge in building a registry of patients beyond existing registries, the most important step in making primary healthcare functional.

When DiNC was finally operational, ASHAs spread out to enrol the locals. From then onward, any interaction they had with the public healthcare system in Kolar added to a clinical medical history that doctors on the system could access. Patients no longer required paper records. Every time they met with or spoke to a doctor on the system, their central health record was updated.

Their records were viewable on an app called the Clinicograph, which provided doctors a comprehensive view of a patient's medical history. The Clinicograph arranged a patient's health data in chronological order, with the most recent reports on top. It was accessible anywhere, by anyone authorized to do so.

From the perspective of patients, it was easy to see the benefits. They did not need to travel long distances to find medical advice, nor did they have to maintain medical reports. They did not have to recall their medical history for a doctor each time. Regardless of where they sat, doctors had access to the same records. Based on what they saw, distant specialists could consult on a course of treatment to local doctors. At a moment's notice, they could find test results, notes by previous doctors, and recordings of conversations—all of which, taken together, could yield vital medical clues. Anything could be relevant, so the Clinicograph's back-end system, the Concentric Data Repository (CDR), vacuumed it all: Maternity cards that patients kept in physical form, scanned images of past doctor prescriptions, test results on paper.

This sort of 'unstructured' information would have been difficult to use in the past. But technology's advances have unlocked new ways of finding meaning. With machine learning and AI, the value in old medical documents can be extracted more easily. Automated processes mine the system's database to understand whether a particular patient has done certain laboratory tests just by 'reading' the scanned images of test documents in the database, and checking for the patient's name and the name of the laboratory test. New technologies allow such 'reading' and 'processing' algorithms at scale, identifying patterns and insights from vast troves of data in a fraction of the time it would take healthcare personnel. It might even—when it is advanced enough—decipher doctors' handwriting.

This analysis of data, repeated thousands of times over a wide geographic area, could potentially understand the ebb and flow of the health of individuals, neighbourhoods, districts and entire countries. It could better understand how citizens seek health, understand what health practices are more effective, provide disease patterns and predict outbreaks, and improve the health system's efficiency by identifying shortages.

The possibilities are endless. The technological platform is receptive to innovation; it is possible to plug in a range of devices and complimentary services. One such invention, a camera backed by AI that assesses images for pre-cancerous lesions within seconds, was plugged into the DiNC's platform. Doctors then took over.

Doctors and other professionals used the platform to provide services, such as Lamaze classes, or educated patients in techniques that were commonplace at high-end urban hospitals, but infinitely rarer in rural India. All of this happened in Kannada, a language local residents understood.

The platform's flexibility also made it easy to scale. Technology innovations at the back-end make light work of the kryptonite of healthcare digitization so far—the array of disparate systems that are used across various healthcare facilities. A single hospital may have a different information system for its patients, its diagnostic laboratory and its radiology department. The platform streamlines the tangle of 'structured data' coming from various legacy health systems, using a combination of medical expertise and technology. The costs, time and effort to implement are estimated to be far lower than that of equivalent approaches—Health Information Exchange technologies, for instance—used in the developed world.

DiNC's technology elements are a harbinger to what is possible when the combination of data, connectivity and AI is deployed in context. But with Bridgital, technology is only part of the story. Truly solving India's healthcare access challenge needs the right mix of people and processes as well.

37

Ubayakushalaopari

To Minister Kumar, the DiNC's approach to healthcare reminded him of a Kannada letter-writing custom before the advent of email. 'Traditionally the first sentence in a letter was, "We are all safe here, we are anxious to know and by the grace of God we believe that you are all safe there."' This was called Ubayakushalaopari, he explained. 'The well-being of both of us.'

Every morning, in the large bright room in the sanatorium that housed the DiNC, nurses, doctors and coordinators sat in silos and phoned people across Kolar. Their workspaces were marked by signs that dangled above: 'DiNC coordinator', 'Mother and childcare coordination', 'DiNC nurse', 'Non-communicable diseases coordination', and 'Speciality care coordination'. The callers wore hospital coats. With their headsets on, and toggling windows on the DiNC platform, they introduced themselves to patients who were mostly pleasantly surprised to be asked after. The callers browsed through the records of each patient, looking up their history in notes that had been written and uploaded. 'Anaemia', some notes were titled, and expanding them presented a more detailed picture. The notes were a guide, a way to catch up and record more information.

Sister Karuna, one of the callers, had been a nursing professor at a college in Bengaluru, and supervised nurses at a local hospital. She joined DiNC in February 2018 on the suggestion of the district health officer, and took to it immediately. She trained ASHAs and coordinated with patients and families to bring them into the system's fold. Karuna had found dealing with patients she could not see disorienting at first, but grew used to the system. Months after she began, when we watched her work at Kolar, she thought nothing of calling up people and chatting with them casually to make them open up. 'At a hospital, you can only serve those who turn up. But the poor mostly don't visit hospitals for several reasons. They think they cannot afford treatment. They are unaware of relevant government schemes. They live very far from large hospitals and losing money and time to visit a hospital does not suit them,' Karuna said.

One of the big challenges of her job, she said, was in helping people overcome their superstitions. 'Sometimes pregnant women tell me that they don't have milk with their coffee. They think it will affect their baby. I tell them that it is nothing like that.' The area was filled with deeply held beliefs about how good health could be attained. The good news, sister Karuna said, was that when she called with medical advice, at least they listened.

The calls were supposed to last no more than ten minutes, but several of them went on for twice as long. With a concerned voice at the other end, people unloaded their questions. Sister Karuna took questions about getting exercise, and informed someone that a government health card would cover their medical expenses. For a family that couldn't afford food with iron, she advised a switch from sugar to jaggery.

'I contacted a pregnant woman in a remote rural area,' she recalled. 'She was severely anaemic and both she and the baby could have been compromised. In addition, the family was opposed to her taking supplements because they feared losing the baby.' Karuna counselled them constantly, eventually bringing them around. 'The woman received treatment for anaemia, and the delivery was safe. At another time, such a patient would have probably died, or left the baby with a slim chance of survival.' Anaemia was a common topic for Karuna, given that one out of two Indian women is anaemic.[1]

The other part of DiNC could be found at Sri Narasimharaja (SNR) district hospital, a crowded facility a few kilometres from the sanatorium. Chanda, in her late twenties and a resident of Bangarpet, a sleepy little town full of fields of ragi and tomato plantations, arrived for work at 9 a.m. Her job, as a patient care coordinator, was to liaise between the various doctors, hospital departments and staff, so that patients moved smoothly and quickly through the hospital. The care coordinators were sorters of a kind. They recorded basic information and guided patients to the right doctors and testing labs. They also maintained order while some patients arrived with referrals and appointments, and others showed up without notice. In their absence, these tasks would have fallen to doctors and nurses, or to informal entrepreneurs like Nikhil Burman.

Mornings were a rush. They began with checking in at DiNC's new videoconferencing facility, which connected SNR's doctors with patients at distant health centres (when Internet connectivity was available). She then toured the wards and OPDs, taking stock of the appointments for the day, and checking the availability of doctors. 'I love my work,' she said. 'Some of the doctors are very strict and you need to check with them before having a word, but some of them are more relaxed. It is great to be able to help patients and to guide them.'

The DiNC job was very different from anything Chanda had done before. 'I like the fact that I have to move around a lot here. I hate being in one place all day. And meeting so many people is the best part of the job.' She walked around with a tablet in her hand, attracting the attention of patients who gave her their details, and allowed themselves to be led by her.

Chanda began as one of six care coordinators who worked at the hospital, each with their own beats to manage. Her salary was ₹12,000 ($170) a month, double what she earned answering calls for a car dealership. Within months, her enthusiasm and capability were widely recognized, and she was promoted to manage and train new patient care coordinators. Six care coordinators now reported to her, and she would be the first person to approach for any escalations within the system.

The promotion came with a salary spike. She now earned ₹18,000 ($260), and was the primary breadwinner of her family. 'Almost 90 per cent of the household expenses are borne by me,' she said proudly.

'We were barely able to make ends meet,' said Chanda. 'But with the promotion, we will now be able to put some money away in savings. I am going to treat my entire family when my first salary as an implementation specialist comes.'

38

Recovery

Shireen Junaid, a mother to two daughters, staggered into a primary health centre in Kolar. She was pregnant, and quite unwell. It was February 2018, and the primary health centre looked nothing like the government medical facilities she knew. The place smelled of new paint. Nurses held electronic tablets. There were rows of metal chairs lined against the walls. A green-coated attendant handed her an appointment slip. Minutes later, she was ushered into a consulting room where a doctor brought up a scanned image of her recent medical history, and wrote down her symptoms. Then the doctor placed a call, and another doctor appeared on a screen behind him.

Dr Kumar, the man on the screen, pulled up Shireen's records. He noticed that her haemoglobin count was already severely low, at 6.40 grams per decilitre, and the delivery was just a few months away. She had a rare blood type—O negative—so finding a donor or supply for a blood transfusion would be difficult. The longer they let her blood count stay low, the greater danger she and the baby would be in.

Kumar recommended that Shireen receive injections of iron—as many doses as they could manage before the delivery. He advised her to visit the district hospital for these injections. Shireen was not interested. She said the hospital made her wait for hours she didn't have. The travel time, on top of the half-day spent jostling to see a doctor, filled Shireen with dread. Her children would have to come along too. Her husband worked two restaurant shifts, and her parents lived hours away.

The doctor assured her that things had changed now, and told her to expect a phone call.

Later that day, a few hours after she left the Kolar centre, her phone rang. The caller asked if they could book her an appointment at the hospital the next day. The approach surprised Shireen, who was unused to being checked on. The next morning, within minutes of entering the hospital, Shireen was sent into a consulting room where a doctor administered an injection. A nurse told her there would be two more. Altogether, she had spent no more than half an hour at the hospital. Shireen grew used to the calls, the people at the other end fixing her appointments for her, reminding her of this or that. Each time she visited the hospital, the speed at which she was served and discharged surprised her. By the time Shireen went into labour, the treatment had worked. Her recovery had been helped in part by encouragement and advice from callers she had never met.

There were other stories too. From Guwahati, a panicked cancer patient barred from boarding a flight home called DiNC with an urgent request for a doctor's note. Within fifteen minutes, DiNC produced a note that allowed him to board the flight. From Chennai, a doctor received a frantic call from a patient driven to thoughts of suicide due to pain. By looking at the patient's Clinicograph, and speaking with the patient, the doctor was able to identify that he had not taken the prescribed pain medication, and duly counselled him to do so.

The stories were validation for a new approach to healthcare—one that emphasized staying in touch with patients. In this system, the effect of well-timed phone calls was crucial. The system did not wait for patients to act on their own; it accounted for human nature, for limitations of time and money. The calls indicated to their recipient that someone was looking out for them, smoothing their visits to doctors and hospitals, removing the hurdles they found so dispiriting. All this was to overcome the deep mistrust patients had of the public healthcare system from which they expected so little.

Slowly but surely, patients turned up at the primary health centres in greater numbers. Between February and July 2018, the primary health facilities covered by DiNC saw a 55 per cent increase in visiting patients from the previous year. By November 2018, more than 500 patients had undergone virtual consultations at public health facilities. On balance, 40 per cent of virtual consultations were to ensure that a patient visiting a primary health centre did not have to return without seeing a doctor, while the rest were to ensure that a patient could consult with a specialist at their nearest health centre, without having to travel to visit a specialist.

The figures were from a single district. But it was enough to provide a glimpse of what was possible.

39

The Bridgital Model

In 2018, we set out to understand the impact of Bridgital on jobs, wages, productivity and access to services in India.

We initially turned to a global study: A McKinsey Global Institute model that quantified the impact of automation on workforces globally.[1] To do this, they first broke down industries into a series of occupations, and each occupation into a series of tasks. They then broke down each task into five sets of skills—physical and manual, basic cognitive, higher cognitive, social and emotional, and technological—and assessed when technology could achieve the capabilities of a worker in a given skill category. Then, they estimated when that technology might become financially viable.

When technologies are able to replicate skills at a low enough cost, specific tasks start to be automated. When most of the tasks within an occupation can be automated, that occupation itself is considered automated. The dependence on the type of skills involved, the level of skill required and worker remuneration, all help explain why sectors automate at a different pace from one another. It's why the progress of automation varies from one economy to the next. While stylized, this reflects quite well the broad thrust of how automation is likely to progress.

In a country where labour is relatively scarce, skilled and so expensive, companies may be early technology adopters, automating large parts of their workforce. On the other hand, in a country like India, it may be a while for technology to be inexpensive enough to compete with the low cost of labour. McKinsey's model estimates that, for India, 9 per cent of current work hours will be automated by 2030—much lower than the 23–24 per cent impact estimated in the US and Germany.

Demystifying Work

We modified this model, applying the Bridgital approach to incorporate what we saw on the ground in India. We saw not a binary choice between automation or no automation. Instead, we saw a world in which work was demystified—disaggregated and redistributed through the aid of the cloud, AI and related technologies. In this world, lower-wage, digitally augmented workers are able to take on tasks previously done only by experts and specialists. This frees up time and capacity for the latter to use their skills optimally. Technology allows the seamless transfer of the freed-up time and capacity—mediated by digitally augmented workers in the last mile—to cater to the needs of the underserved. The result is an enhanced system since the specialized workers focus on what they do best and other workers take on new, more productive tasks. Most importantly, it is more inclusive.

The right tools could take a load off junior doctors, nurses and health associates. Many pre-diagnosis activities, for instance, could be turned into a checklist programmed onto a kiosk, a handheld tablet, or even a smartphone, and then be used by someone without clinical training. The data they collect could be analysed almost instantly by medical software, and be made available for a doctor to consult whenever they wanted. The software could be programmed to highlight potential problems, signal improvements, or even suggest treatment approaches.

Specialist doctors are able to conduct virtual consultations with patients well beyond where roads end, where the choice to access healthcare is a major life decision. This is where the benefits of the Bridgital approach meet the road.

Bridgital Addresses India's Twin Challenges of Jobs and Access: The Healthcare Example[2]

Shifting and Automating Tasks Free Doctors and Create Work; Deploying It Remotely Improves Access and Creates Jobs

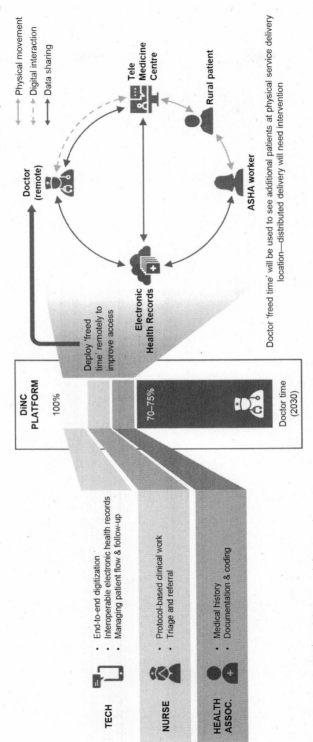

Physical movement
Digital interaction
Data sharing

Tele Medicine Centre

Rural patient

Doctor (remote)

ASHA worker

Electronic Health Records

DiNC PLATFORM

100%

Deploy 'freed time' remotely to improve access

70–75%

Doctor time (2030)

TECH
- End-to-end digitization
- Interoperable electronic health records
- Managing patient flow & follow-up

NURSE
- Protocol-based clinical work
- Triage and referral

HEALTH ASSOC.
- Medical history
- Documentation & coding

Doctor 'freed time' will be used to see additional patients at physical service delivery location—distributed delivery will need intervention

Source: Tata Sons and McKinsey & Company analysis

Bridgital Healthcare

India currently has about 700,000 practising doctors. To reach a standard considered acceptable by the World Health Organisation, it will need more than it can currently produce. By 2030, when it will need a bare minimum of 1.5 million doctors, there will instead be just over a million.[3]

By our estimate, a Bridgital transformation of the entire Indian public health system—automating and reassigning tasks—could free up the equivalent of 370,000 full-time doctors by 2030.[4] Added to this, Bridgital approaches could create a million new jobs in healthcare, and make another million more productive. With gains in productivity will come wage gains—on average, digitally augmented workers should see a 15–20 per cent rise in their wages.

Bridgital Notably Addresses the Doctor Supply Gap

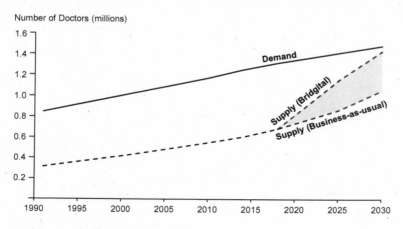

Number of Doctors (millions)

Source: Tata Sons and McKinsey & Company analysis

40

Bridgital More Broadly

The transformations at AIIMS and Kolar are real-world demonstrations of applying Bridgital in healthcare. But the principles that underpin Bridgital can be applied anywhere, by anyone, at any time. We discuss a few sectors below and in the charts on the following pages.

Agriculture: If agriculture, the source of livelihood for nearly half of India's workforce, underwent a Bridgital makeover, it would centre around agriculture extension workers. The traditional role of an extension worker has been to disseminate new knowledge to farmers.[1] These workers have the advantage of local language and dialect, coupled with knowledge of specific cultural contexts. However, low penetration rates and vacancies limit the potential impact of the extension worker role today.

For extension workers, the transformation could be in the form of digital platforms that offer information and farming insights based on granular data—things farmers currently lack access to, limiting their productivity. Roles would change here too. Extension workers could collect data by testing soil and water. They could help farmers sign on to online marketplaces that offer everything from credit to trucks. Depending on how many of India's 1.6–1.7 million farm holdings adopt agricultural services, augmented extension workers could range between 500,000 to one million in number.[2]

Logistics: A Bridgital approach in logistics would make the perilous job of a truck driver simpler, safer and more productive. A platform could train drivers, insure them, remind them of safety measures, provide real-time guidance on routes and driving behaviour and direct them to the nearest place where they could get a good night's sleep. It would also include infrastructure that makes this a reality, such as rest stops with proper food, sanitation and dormitory facilities in critical locations.

Platforms would turn long-distance transport into a relay-type task, breaking up a cross-country journey into multiple day-long trips by a succession of drivers. And yet things would move faster: Truck fleets would be on the road continuously, reducing transit time by 50 per cent or more.[3]

Judiciary: A Bridgital effect on the judiciary would make more efficient use of judges' time, lowering the 30-50 per cent of time taken up by administrative and procedural hearings. Augmented 'courtroom managers' could help reduce the workload of judges and also tide over the 5,800 courtroom vacancies currently. Records would be digitized, case summaries would be supported by AI, and courts would know instantly if the same case was being heard by courts in different locations.

If the spectrum of transformation includes agriculture, logistics, the judiciary, education, and financial services as well, we believe that a Bridgital approach will directly impact 30 million workers by 2025—in the form of new jobs, as well as augments to existing ones. Wages for these workers will likely increase around 10-20 per cent. It will expand the size of the formal economy. At the same time, more than 200 million citizens will experience improved access to services.[4]

Bridgital: 30 Million Gainful Jobs,
across Six Sectors by 2025

HEALTHCARE

- **Bridgital workers:** Allied Health Professionals and ASHA workers
- **Augment:** Protocols, tools & templates for shifted tasks; platform based interoperable clinical information; real-time resource and equipment availability
- **Process & role changes:** Shift from 'care-only' to 'care-coordination' and from point care to a continuum of care; shifting and automation of low-value tasks; remote delivery of care via expert consultations
- **Value creation:** $15–20 billion additional value-added by 2025 from greater worker productivity, due to fewer sick days and fewer days lost to access healthcare

National Priority: Ayushman Bharat

JOBS IMPACTED	WAGE INCREMENT	CITIZENS WITH BETTER ACCESS
1–2 mn	**15–20%**	**200–300 mn**
ASHAs & allied health professionals		Patients

Source: Tata Group Pilots; Tata Sons and McKinsey & Company analysis

EDUCATION

- **Bridgital workers:** Teachers and teaching assistants
- **Augment:** Automation and shifting of administrative tasks; AI-based tools to diagnose learning achievement and provide remedial instruction; novel pedagogical content
- **Process & role changes:** Effective shift of system from age-grade to learning-grade; institutionalized teacher training and curriculum standardization
- **Value creation:** $25–70 billion additional value-added by 2025 from higher wages earned by students' effective 1 to 3 year boost in years of education from better learning outcomes

National Priority: Education for All

JOBS IMPACTED	WAGE INCREMENT	CITIZENS WITH BETTER ACCESS
10–12 mn	–	**200–250 mn**
Teachers		Students

Source: Tata Sons and McKinsey & Company analysis

Bridgital More Broadly

AGRICULTURE

- **Bridgital workers:** Farm extension workers
- **Augment:** Precision farming advisory; AI-based support for risk assessment, underwriting; link to online marketplaces
- **Process & role changes:** Platform-based centralization of tasks done by different agents in the ecosystem—market intermediation for agricultural products and transport, guidance for crop and livestock growing, insurance
- **Value creation:** $30–35 billion additional value-added by 2025 through improvements in yields

National Priority: Doubling farmers' income

JOBS IMPACTED	WAGE INCREMENT	CITIZENS WITH BETTER ACCESS
0.5–1 mn	–	**100–200 mn**
Farm extension workers		Farmers

LOGISTICS

- **Bridgital workers:** Commercial vehicle drivers
- **Augment:** Real-time feedback on driving behaviour, route and load optimization; improved utilization
- **Process & role changes:** Shift to relay, 'always-on' model; greater formalization through platform-based demand-and-supply matching; accompanying improvements in safety and quality through formalization
- **Value creation:** $6–8 billion additional value-added by 2025 from reduced turn-around time for intercity goods movement

National Priority: Make in India

JOBS IMPACTED	WAGE INCREMENT	CITIZENS WITH BETTER ACCESS
12–15 mn	**10–15%**	–
Goods transport drivers		Businesses

Source: Tata Sons and McKinsey & Company analysis

Bridgital Nation

FINANCIAL SERVICES

- **Bridgital workers:** Business correspondents (BCs)
- **Augment:** Real-time identity verification; AI-based support for risk assessment, underwriting for loans and insurance
- **Process & role changes:** Platform-based centralization of tasks done by different parties in the ecosystem—targeting and identification of underserved, service extension and customization
- **Value creation:** $15–20 billion additional value-added by 2025 from lower cash usage in the rural economy (substantial further benefits from greater rural credit provision and penetration of micro-insurance and micro-pension services not estimated)

National Priority: Jan Dhan Yojana, Direct Benefits

JOBS IMPACTED	WAGE INCREMENT	CITIZENS WITH BETTER ACCESS
0.5–1 mn	**10–15%**	**200–400 mn**
Business correspondents		Unbanked/ dormant

JUDICIARY

- **Bridgital workers:** Judges and courtroom managers
- **Augment:** Case management tools, including evidence gathering, dashboards to track case progress, searchable case and document records
- **Process & role changes:** Standardization of procedures, protocols to enable transferring procedures to platform, intermediate worker or technology-generated case summaries
- **Value creation:** $2–3 billion in GVA by 2025 from lower earnings loss for litigants enabled by speedier case resolution (substantial further benefits—freeing up assets for economic activity; fewer undertrials not estimated)

National Priority: Right to Justice

JOBS IMPACTED	WAGE INCREMENT	CITIZENS WITH BETTER ACCESS
10–20,000	–	**100–150 mn**
Judges & courtroom managers		Citizens

Source: Tata Sons and McKinsey & Company analysis

These are conservative estimates, and cautious numbers. Bridgital isn't a miraculous solution. It's a leap from where we are, and a step towards where we could be. These numbers speak of the slow, painstaking, yet ultimately rewarding path of incremental change that lies ahead as the future of work becomes our present.

•—•

So how can India make it possible for everyone, no matter where they are, to apply Bridgital principles?

To begin with, data privacy—the foundation of any Bridgital approach—is a necessity. India is in the process of recognizing individuals' right over their personal data. As it does this, it needs to ensure that data can be accessed only by people who are authorized to do so, but without stifling researchers who need it. At the same time, India requires an authority that can provide redress for unauthorized access to data. There's a range of models to pick from: The China model, which restricts most forms of access; the US model, where firms set the terms on which they access data; and the EU model, which is conservative but balanced.

Second, industries and organizations would benefit from freedom to experiment with existing roles and create new ones. For example, there are certain tasks that only doctors are permitted to do, such as prescribing certain drugs, and

243

administering life-saving injections. This is something an advanced nurse practitioner—a role already mainstreamed by the National Health Service in the UK—could do just as well. What's needed is some more lightness of touch when India limits what its professionals are permitted to do.

Third, technology can help overcome old apprehensions by redefining how services are delivered. Currently, a doctor must be physically present in the same room as the patient to write them a prescription. In another time, this was a precaution against fake prescriptions being used to create a black market in prescription medication. Now, with digital signatures and remote consultations becoming the norm, the precaution is a hurdle to better ways of functioning. There are very likely similar instances of well-meaning regulations in other industries that have outlived their purpose.

Fourth, digital skilling needs official recognition. By certifying the knowledge that augmented workers gain in the course of their work, India will encourage its people to improve their skills, knowledge, and productivity. This feeds into a virtuous cycle where workers will build on technical knowledge and twenty-first-century skills, such as collaboration and creativity. When it comes to twenty-first-century skills, we need to design our educational approach in new ways. Creativity, for instance, is a natural human tendency—but we can study the circumstances under which it flourishes, and design our educational system in ways that offer such opportunities to every student. Collaboration, which appears like a basic task, can be perceived as progression through stages of learning and mastery over dozens of skills including negotiation and conflict resolution. Critical thinking requires a change in mindset, from passive transmission of knowledge to learning by questioning and testing hypotheses.

Reaching this state will involve novel approaches, like the use of regulatory sandboxes—experimental settings where new rules are tested, their impact studied, and then used to formulate new policies for the entire sector. At the same time, the shaping of data rules must be as collaborative as possible, with the participation of all stakeholders— start-ups, academia, civil society, small and large private companies.

The world over, countries are grappling with ideas about data and responsibility, hoping to find some kind of balance. If India can create a regime forged from the concerns of every stakeholder, it won't just be a shining light unto itself—it will illuminate a path for others too.

Conclusion

India's challenges are urgent. It is easy to be trapped in crisis mode, fighting fires as they spring up. To evolve, though, the country has to anticipate and actively design the future it wants.

To do this, three transformations lie ahead. The first is a technological transformation, in which India develops the capacity of advanced digital tools to address its great challenges. The second is a talent transformation, which will equip its students and workers with the ability to enhance themselves and their prospects through technological augmentation. The third—and perhaps the most important—is a transformation of vision: Rather than muddling through existing constraints, India needs to position itself as a pioneer shaping the future of work.

Technology

Too many conversations about how technology will affect the workplace are based on false binaries: human or machine, replace or retain. How India applies technology is a choice. Rather than debating whether (or when) AI will grow smarter than humans, it should instead think deeply about the implications of this most apparent fact: The combination of human and AI will certainly be smarter and more effective than either human or AI alone. Countries that develop smart systems look to derive and refine insights from their data, and tap into the power of technology and data combined to build contextual solutions that meet their needs.

India is going through a rapid expansion in connectivity. As more and more Indians come online, the volume of data being generated will make it possible to contextualize and customize solutions with greater precision. The development of applications and technologies for use in the last mile in India requires, among other things, a period of testing. Machine learning algorithms, in particular, will show remarkable improvements in performance as they are allowed to work through successive iterations.

The kinds of technologies India needs to develop will focus on what we have called Bridgital solutions: Rather than aiming to replace human workers, these will look to interact with humans in ways that are mutually complementary.

Many elements of context are inherently familiar to humans, but beyond the capacity of AI at this time; conversely, once a task has been structured and set up in a predictable manner, digital technologies are able to do the task quicker and more reliably than the average human.

Combining these two capacities is at the heart of the Bridgital strategy, and will help design locally relevant and applicable solutions. In a country with a vast pool of job-seekers at every level of skill, and with the persistent gaps in access that we have examined, India should focus on how Bridgital combinations of data, connectivity and AI can be deployed to address its twin challenges. In the book, we describe this process of tech-innovation-led delivery as 'scoring a hat-trick': We will provide last-mile consumers with access to basic services at low cost, we will generate millions of jobs while doing so, and these jobs will prepare the workforce of the future for the workplace of the future.

Talent

India is a vast pool of untapped human resources. It hasn't leveraged this resource as reliably or on the scale that it needs to. Beyond basic literacy and numeracy, India needs to design an education system based on five principles: digital skills; twenty-first-century skills (creativity, collaboration and critical thinking); new-age apprenticeships; lifelong learning; and entrepreneurial thinking.

Digital skills are going to be a baseline expectation in the workplace of the future. Much as reading, writing and counting are taught as basic skills that underpin all other learning, today's students must be trained in how to navigate the Internet and Fourth Industrial Revolution fields. The ability to seek out information using digital tools, to filter what one finds and identify what is most relevant to one's purposes, and to adapt and apply that material to real-world questions will be central to all forms of learning and work hereafter.

Building twenty-first-century skills is easier said than done. To dismiss these as 'soft' skills is a vast underestimation of the effort that goes into nurturing them. The good news is that these skills—such as creativity, collaboration and critical thinking—can be nurtured. The concepts can be introduced in early years and blended into other curricula; students can then be given opportunities to practise, all the way up to adolescence, with increasingly deliberate attention to the skill. Developing these skills means giving students the opportunity to experiment with real-world problems. Not only does this encourage contextual learning and application, but it also lets them experience failure—a key element in learning how to learn, test, iterate and persevere.

Conclusion

Apprenticeships (broadly defined as structured learning-by-doing opportunities, typically under the supervision and guidance of a professional) are central to making the things one learns—including twenty-first-century skills—practical and relevant to the workplace. In addition to becoming familiar with a professional field and learning to apply one's skills in that space, apprenticeships will also boost employability—especially if combined with a certification scheme that provides a credible signal to prospective employers about an apprentice's practical training and abilities.

The rapidly changing nature of both technology and work processes in the future workplace puts a premium on lifelong learning. To take advantage of the latest advancements, and to explore new fields as they open, people will have to regularly and systematically devote time and effort to upgrading their skills. In a labour market with a large number of job-seekers, it is neither efficient nor fair to place the burden of this task solely on individuals; rather, India has to think about expanding its education system in ways that will support workers and employers by offering opportunities for lifelong learning.

Finally, India will have to nurture the attitudinal aspects of entrepreneurship. An entrepreneurial mindset—the willingness to take on risks, and the skills to assess these risks and opportunities wisely—has never been a priority in education. For all the recent changes in examination and retention policies, failure is still a stigma.

The education system is designed for the industrial age: A nineteenth-century apparatus that India expects will create twenty-first-century problem-solvers. India must change this to a system that provides the scaffolding for skills a future workforce will require, with opportunities for learning, unlearning and relearning at every age and stage of professional life.

Designing pathways to productive work for both women and men will be necessary. Only by transforming how India thinks about human capacity and talent can it establish itself as a truly smart nation.

Vision

As if India's existing challenges were not enough, it also has to confront the increasingly rapid pace of change. This is a global trend; India is yet to experience its full impact, partly because infrastructure and connectivity vary to such a great extent across the country. None of us can precisely predict the tipping point. Once it takes off, tech-driven disruption will unfold at an exponential rate. Countries, industries and companies that are unprepared will forever struggle to catch up.

What can India do? India can anticipate this trajectory. It has already led the way for the world to reimagine ways of work once, during the transition from hardware to software. In that process, it has learned much about what it takes to integrate technology and humans, and create ever more resilient and effective workplaces. Now, India's goal must be the seamless integration of human capacities, digital tools and AI.

When electricity was first introduced into industrial processes, it required thousands, if not millions, of micro-innovations—people tinkering around the margins, finding new ways to apply this new power source to reshape their factories and industries. So too with computers: The process of computerizing work across everything from hospitals to banks to airlines required experimentation and adaptation.

India can cultivate the same pioneering mindset when it comes to Bridgital technologies today. A given platform or stack has the potential to transform an industry, but it will be the imagination of the early adopters that determines how that potential is deployed.

India will need to build bridges. It grapples with many 'missing middles' every day—the mid-skill jobs it isn't creating; the secondary-educated women who aren't in the workforce; the mid-sized firms that so few Indian start-ups grow into. India's job is to build those middles: to build the bridges between talent and productive work, using technology and foresight.

Reinvention is never easy. One must devise an entirely new way of working, without the reassurance that comes with replicating already existing best practices. This isn't just about finding new applications for the technology: India needs to anticipate its impact as well—the risks and disruptions it can bring. Yet this is precisely how every previous transformation has played out, and it is this attitude of flexibility, courage and judicious risk-taking that will let India be on the forefront of the Fourth Industrial Revolution.

⁕——⁕

The fact is that the twin challenges will not fix themselves. Nor will India be able to address them at scale if it continues on its usual course. Jugaad, tweaks and tricks, can only take it so far.

This is why Bridgital is the next big opportunity for India, and one it cannot afford to miss. It is the development that will let India unlock its vast pool of talent, and apply their capacities to addressing the most inextricable problems of these times. In putting these solutions in place, it is assured of a pipeline of twenty-first-century talent for decades ahead. The three strategies we describe in the book can harness the potential of both, technologies and talent, and use them to make life better for every Indian.

Conclusion

Smart policy can play a role in each of the three transformations:

Technology: The government can invest substantially in research and development, while also building a legal and regulatory ecosystem that encourages innovation, especially in the Bridgital field. India needs a wave of new entrepreneurs who can adapt technologies for its needs, and the government can provide them both the room and the incentives to experiment.

Talent: The reimagining of India's education system, from its current industrial focus to one that nurtures agile and digitally native problem-solvers, is the greatest investment any government can make for India's future. Education reform will not be easy, given how large and entrenched the current system is—yet it could not be any more urgent.

Vision: Any new vision of the workplace must emphasize flexibility, adaptability and mobility. This requires new policies and legal systems that can work with workers— protecting and supporting people as they explore careers through diagonal moves from one firm or industry to another.

The sheer scope of India's challenges means that there is room for everyone to work on addressing them. Public– private partnerships—and indeed, even reforms of public service delivery systems such as healthcare, education and the judiciary—are precisely how these innovations will be incorporated and institutionalized.

If all of this sounds daunting, keep in mind that the scale and complexity of India's challenges is itself an opportunity. Unlike a more developed but less populous or less diverse country, India has both the urgency and the human resources. When India does crack these challenges, the solutions it devises will be relevant to many other societies and countries.

The future of work will be imagined, designed, tested, and made in India. We have all the tools, and we've already tested the waters.

Let's dive in.

To share ideas and feedback on the themes in this book, write to bridgital@tata.com.

Acknowledgements

FROM N. CHANDRASEKARAN

Over the past three decades, my career at TCS gave me the opportunity to understand how technology can impact businesses. In the Indian context, I have been able to see how the digitization of systems, such as passport issuance and income tax filing, has made a significant impact on the public as well. My colleagues at TCS and many of our customers helped me understand the power of technology in different situations. All of these experiences have contributed in various ways to the overarching idea of Bridgital as a means to address large and cross-cutting challenges, an idea I have been nurturing over the past five years.

I must thank Roopa, my co-author, who joined me in this journey of writing *Bridgital Nation* and developing the themes throughout.

Acknowledgements

I would like to thank Mr Ratan Tata for being an inspiration. He sets a precedent for visionary ideas, coupled with an unwavering set of values. He has embodied the Tatas' pioneering spirit of building what the country needs, even when it is a difficult path to pursue.

For being an enormous source of strength, my thanks every day to my wife, Lalitha.

FROM BOTH THE AUTHORS

From the very beginning, this book has been a collaborative effort. Joshua Abraham led the research and analysis for the entire book. Rahul Bhatia edited and contributed with a critical eye to the argument and sound judgement on the writing process. Our thanks to Vishal Vaibhaw, Ameya Ashok Naik, Sumana Guha Ray, Anindya Roy, Nivedita Rao, Naman Narain and Caroline Vincent from the Tata macro research team for their involvement in every chapter—from numbers to documentation to research and interviews.

Thanks to the Penguin India team for their guidance throughout the making of this book, in particular our editors, Meru Gokhale and Richa Burman.

We are grateful to everyone who reviewed the manuscript. Special thanks to Dominic Wilson, R.K. Krishna Kumar, Gaurav Gupta, Harish Bhat and Pradipta Bagchi for valuable feedback.

Acknowledgements

Unnati Tripathi, Tanya Loh, the TCS team in Kolar and Arjun Sharma of 101Reporters in Punjab contributed to the various narratives throughout the book. Partha P. Chakrabartty helped articulate some of the ideas in The Bridgital Transformation and implications for the future of work in India. We would also like to thank Katherine Boo for her guidance.

Vivek Pandit, Anu Madgavkar, Shishir Gupta and Himanshu Satija of McKinsey & Company worked closely with us to project the impact of Bridgital. Swetha Totapally, Kishan Shah, Patrick Quigley, Karishma Attari, Pritham Raja, Nergish Sunavala and Shreya Menon of Dalberg Advisors contributed to the chapters 'XX Factor—The Talent Dividend' and 'Everywhere Entrepreneurship'.

For sharing perspectives, we are grateful to Dr Devi Shetty, Dr M.C. Misra, Dr G.N. Saxena, Dr C.S. Pramesh, Roshika Singh, Ravi Poddar, Sairee Chahal, Ashutosh Tandon, Anant Ahuja, Josh Foulger, Shashi Kalathil, Lisa Heydlauff, Clement Chauvet, and doctors and staff of the Cachar Cancer Hospital & Research Centre.

We made every effort to represent the data and our findings accurately. Any errors are our own.

We thank the Tata family. We worked closely with the TCS teams, led by Girish Krishnamurthy, that run DiNC in Kolar and other parts of India. Venguswamy Ramaswamy and his team at TCS iON shared valuable

259

insight and experience. N.G. Subramaniam, COO of TCS, was a generous source of TCS institutional history. Tata STRIVE, Tata Global Beverages Limited and Tata Steel Limited provided much-needed assistance to our research on the ground. Project teams and sector experts at Tata Trusts offered unique insights from years of experience in the field. Various departments of Tata Sons Private Limited including Corporate Communications, Digital, HR, Legal, and the Company Secretary's office provided timely and vital support. The Indian Hotels Company Limited showed us their legendary care and attention to detail on our many trips across the country. In our fieldwork, so many people and organizations welcomed us simply because the Tatas have been a part of their own history. The trust that the Tata Group has built over more than a century is truly unparalleled.

This book would not have been possible without the stories we were able to capture in each chapter. Our collaborators, across India, welcomed us into their homes and communities, fed us, shared their hopes, fears, criticisms and wisdom, and then fed us some more. The warmth, hospitality and sense of urgency was both palpable and common throughout the country. We came away with far more than a narrative. Thank you.

Notes

INTRODUCTION

1. Peter Diamandis, 'Is Tech Unemployment Good or Bad?', *Forbes*, 14 July 2014. Available at: https://www.forbes.com/sites/peterdiamandis/2014/07/14/is-tech-unemployment-good-or-bad/#3159a9184eb7

2. D.S. Brown Jr, 'The Automobile Question [Letter to the Editor]', *The New York Times*, 03 July 1899. Available at: https://nyti.ms/2ZbZeTW

3. The Fourth Industrial Revolution (4IR) is the current and developing environment in which disruptive technologies and trends such as the Internet of Things (IoT), robotics, virtual reality (VR), autonomous transport and artificial intelligence (AI) are changing the way we live and work. The term was coined by Klaus Schwab, Founder, World Economic Forum.

    The First Industrial Revolution, in the late eighteenth and nineteenth centuries, involved a change from mostly agrarian societies to greater industrialization; the Second Industrial Revolution was driven by electricity and involved expansion of industries and mass production; and the Third Industrial Revolution involved the development of computers and IT since the middle of the twentieth century.

4. Tim Dean, 'The mind of Michio Kaku', *Cosmos Magazine*, 21 July 2014. Available at: https://cosmosmagazine.com/social-sciences/mind-michio-kaku

5. All figures sourced from 'World Population Prospects – 2017 Revision', *UN DESA*. Available at: https://www.un.org/development/desa/publications/graphic/wpp2017-global-population. The medium fertility variant was used for calculation of age-group-wise projections. For India, UN population growth rates were applied to the 2011 census population.

There are multiple definitions of working-age population. We adopt the convention that people aged fifteen years and above are considered to be of working age. More detail can be found in 'The Jobs Challenge'.

6. Analysis by Tata Sons Private Limited ('Tata Sons') using data from 'World Economic Outlook', International Monetary Fund, 2019. Available at: https://www.imf.org/en/Publications/WEO. GDP and GDP per capita statistics are expressed in 2018 US$. An exchange rate of ₹70 per US$ is used throughout the book.

7. India's diversity is legendary. In the words of economist Joan Robinson, 'Whatever you can rightly say about India, the opposite is also true.' Take languages alone: According to the Registrar General and Census Commissioner, more than 19,500

languages and dialects are spoken across the country, with 121 languages spoken by 10,000 or more people. Or consider demography: Some states in the southern part of India are aging faster than some countries in Europe, while in states like Bihar and Uttar Pradesh, fertility rates are over three children per woman. When it comes to politics, the country has over 1,800 state and national parties. Before the recent introduction of the Goods and Services Tax (GST), a commodity could be subject to as many as twenty-two different state taxes as it moved across state borders. Heterogeneity has implications for consumer markets as well. Tata Global Beverages sells thirty-five varieties of tea across the country; the flagship brand, Tata Tea Premium, alone has thirteen different blends customized for regional palates.

8. Tata Sons analysis using data from the IMF and CEIC; 'World Economic Outlook', International Monetary Fund, 2019. Available at: https://www.imf.org/en/Publications/WEO

9. 'Diversity Underlying Unity: The state of India's states: 2018', International Market Assessment Private Limited. Available at: https://www.ima-india.com/templates/imaindia/report_pdf/Diversity%20Underlying%20Unity.pdf

10. Average firm size in India as of 2014 was 2.24. See 'All India Report of Sixth Economic Census', Central Statistics Office, Ministry of Statistics and Programme Implementation, 2014. Available at: http://www.mospi.gov.in/all-india-report-sixth-economic-census

11. Aadhaar is India's massive biometric identification programme. The database is tapped about 20 million times a day for everything from direct government welfare transfers to

opening bank accounts (which now takes just minutes to authenticate, among the fastest in the world).

12. 'National Family Health Survey (NFHS-4)', Ministry of Health and Family Welfare, 2015-16. Available at: http://rchiips.org/nfhs/NFHS-4Reports/India.pdf

13. Tata Sons analysis using data from 'World Economic Outlook', International Monetary Fund, 2019. Available at: https://www.imf.org/en/Publications/WEO.GDP

14. Dominic Wilson and Roopa Purushothaman, 'Dreaming with BRICs: The Path to 2050', Global Economics Paper No: 99, Goldman Sachs, 2003

15. While India has made remarkable progress in reducing absolute poverty, a large part of its population still lives on less than $5 per day.

16. 'Annual Report Periodic Labour Force Survey (PLFS) July 2017–June 2018', Ministry of Statistics and Programme Implementation (MOSPI) and National Statistical Office (NSO), Government of India, May 2019. Available at: http://mospi.nic.in/sites/default/files/publication_reports/Annual%20Report%2C%20PLFS%202017-18_31052019.pdf

    This report is referred to as 'PLFS 2017–18' for the rest of the book.

17. Dani Rodrik, 'The Good Jobs Challenge', Project Syndicate, 7 February, 2019. Available at: https://www.project-syndicate.org/commentary/how-countries-can-create-middle-class-jobs-by-dani-rodrik-2019-02?barrier=accesspaylog

18. Website of the Good Jobs Institute. Available at https://goodjobsinstitute.org/what-is-a-good-job/

19. PLFS 2017–18.

20. According to McKinsey Global Institute's 2014 paper, 'From Poverty to Empowerment: India's imperative for jobs, growth and effective basic services', people in India lack access to 46 per cent of the services they need to fulfil their requirements for an acceptable standard of living. These include healthcare, education, energy and water, and sanitation. Available at: https://www.mckinsey.com/~/media/mckinsey/featured%20insights/asia%20pacific/indias%20path%20from%20poverty%20to%20empowerment/from_poverty_to_empowerment_indias_imperative_for_jobs_growth_and_effective_basic_services_executive_summary.ashx

21. Estimates based on analysis by Tata Sons from various sources.

22. 'Statement showing Approved Strength, Working Strength and Vacancies of Judges in the Supreme Court of India and the High Courts', Department of Justice, Ministry of Law & Justice, 01 July 2019. Available at: http://doj.gov.in/sites/default/files/Vacancy%20%2801.07.2019%29.pdf; Rajya Sabha Unstarred Question No. 2153, answered by the Ministry of Law & Justice on 11 July 2019. Available at: https://rajyasabha.nic.in/rsnew/Questions/QResult.aspx

23. See 'Interim budget 2019-20', Ministry of Finance, Government of India. Available at: https://www.indiabudget.gov.in/ for the proposal to streamline clearances for the film industry. Boosting the textile and garment industries has been a consistent focus of government. For instance, the 'Economic Survey 2016-17', Ministry of Finance, Government of India, had an entire chapter titled, 'Clothes and Shoes: Can India

Reclaim Low Skill Manufacturing?' Available at: https://www.
indiabudget.gov.in/budget2017-2018/es2016-17/echap07.pdf

24. Estimations based on analysis by Tata Sons and McKinsey and
Company. See the section 'Bridgital in Action', for more detail.

25. Referring to XX chromosomes (used in a 2006 Everstone
Capital study, authored by Roopa Purushothaman).

26. Based on analysis done by Tata Sons and Dalberg Advisors
('Dalberg'). See the section 'XX Factor—The Talent
Dividend', for more detail.

27. Micro enterprises employ less than ten people; small enterprises
employ between ten and fifty; and medium enterprises
employ between fifty and 250. Self-employed individuals
(that is, those who have no additional employees) are also
considered micro enterprises. Estimate of the share of private
sector employment in SMEs is based on analysis by Tata Sons
and Dalberg. The benchmark SME share of private sector
employment is based on OECD data for 2014. Countries
included in the benchmark set are Brazil, Czech Republic,
Hungary, Israel, Poland, Romania and Turkey. See the
section 'Everywhere Entrepreneurship', for more detail.

28. Based on analysis done by Tata Sons and Dalberg. See the
section 'Everywhere Entrepreneurship', for more detail.

29. The Tata Group's companies reach 600 million people
every year, and Tata Trusts is among India's oldest and
most established philanthropic organizations. The group
implements projects on health, livelihoods, literacy, water,
sustainability, culture and governance. It also funds research
and analysis on a range of topics from India's languages to
how Indians save and spend, and how they work.

CHAPTER 2: PLAYING ROLES

1. Tripura is a small, remote state in the north-east of India. The third smallest of India's twenty-nine states, it is bounded on three sides by the neighbouring country of Bangladesh. Silchar, the nearest Indian city to Tripura's capital of Agartala, is twice the distance compared to Bangladesh's capital city of Dhaka.

CHAPTER 3: WRAPPING TECHNOLOGY AROUND PEOPLE

1. The Pradhan Mantri Jan Dhan Yojana (PMJDY), launched in 2014, is an ambitious financial inclusion initiative that targets universal access to basic financial services. The programme provides affordable access to no-frills savings bank accounts, credit, insurance and pension facilities. Headline results have been impressive with nearly 80 per cent of adults estimated to have bank accounts as of 2017, up from 53 per cent in 2014. However, 48 per cent of these accounts did not register a transaction in the preceding year. This may perhaps be on account of insufficient time for the newly included to access and use their accounts. Data sourced from the 2017 World Bank Global Findex Database.

2. Amolo Ng'weno et al., 'Let's Be Real: The Informal Sector and the Gig Economy Are the Future, and the Present, of Work in Africa', Centre for Global Development, 2018. Available at: https://www.cgdev.org/publication/lets-be-real-informal-sector-and-gig-economy-are-future-and-present-work-africa

3. For details on doctor density, please see the explanation in the 'The Access Challenge'.

Hospital beds (per 1,000 people), World Health Organisation. Available at: https://data.worldbank.org/indicator/SH.MED. BEDS.ZS?most_recent_value_desc=false

India's skew between urban and rural: 'Report on healthcare access initiatives', KPMG and the Organisation of Pharmaceutical Producers of India, August 2016. Available at: https://www.indiaoppi.com/sites/default/files/PDF%20 files/Report%20on%20healthcare%20access%20 initiatives%20%28For%20web%29.pdf

4. All figures sourced from 'World Population Prospects – 2017 Revision', *UN DESA*. Available at: https://www. un.org/development/desa/publications/graphic/wpp2017-global-population. The medium fertility variant was used for projections.

5. Between 1900 and 1920, electricity saw rapid adoption, going from 5 per cent of business usage to more than 50 per cent in 1920. Adoption reached 75 per cent by 1935. Between 1920 and 1935, productivity growth was nearly five times higher than the average from 1900 to 1920. For a detailed treatment see Zaki Wahhaj and Martin Brookes, 'Is the Internet Better Than Electricity?', Goldman Sachs Global Economics Paper No: 49, 2000.

6. Vasudevan Mukunth, 'Instead of Reaching the Sky, Aakash Ends Up Six Feet Below', *The Wire*, 15 July 2015. Available at: https://thewire.in/education/instead-of-reaching-the-sky-aakash-ends-up-six-feet-below

7. H. James Wilson and Paul Daugherty, 'Collaborative Intelligence: Humans and AI Are Joining Forces', *Harvard Business Review*, July–August 2018. Available at: https://hbr.org/2018/07/collaborative-intelligence-humans-and-ai-are-joining-forces
8. Ibid.

CHAPTER 4: CALCULATIONS

1. Swagata Yadavar and Ojaswi Rao, 'Bankrupt, Poorly Educated, Desperate: Cancer Patients on Mumbai Footpath', *IndiaSpend*, 5 September 2017. Available at: https://archive.indiaspend.com/cover-story/bankrupt-poorly-educated-desperate-cancer-patients-on-mumbai-footpath-54419
2. 'Tracking Universal Health Coverage: 2017 Global Monitoring Report', World Bank, 13 December 2017. Available at: http://www.worldbank.org/en/topic/universalhealthcoverage/publication/tracking-universal-health-coverage-2017-global-monitoring-report

CHAPTER 5: THE GREAT MEDICAL MIGRATION

1. World Bank, World Development Indicators. The phrase 'communicable diseases' is shorthand for communicable, maternal, neonatal and nutritional diseases (CMNNDs).
2. India's public healthcare system has three levels—primary, secondary and tertiary. Broadly, these levels offer patients access to healthcare of increasing sophistication and

specialization. Primary care is the first level of contact, providing basic and essential services. For instance, this includes the treatment of common diseases or injuries, mother-and-child services such as immunization and family planning, and preventive interventions for locally endemic diseases. Primary care is administered through a network of sub-centres and primary health centres (PHCs) spread throughout the country. Secondary care offers more specialized services and, ideally, is supposed to be accessed via referral from primary care. It is administered through hospitals located in the capital of a particular district, and community health centres (CHCs) at the level of a 'block' (administrative units smaller than districts). Tertiary care has specialized medical personnel and offers advanced services, such as intensive care and surgeries. Tertiary care facilities are typically located in towns and cities, or large district capitals. They often function as medical colleges and advanced research institutes as well.

3. The Tata Trusts have pioneered cancer care and research since the 1940s, and recognize the need to shift focus from curative to preventive programmes for early cancer detection. The Trusts envision a distributed cancer control model to create patient-centric cancer centres for delivering uniform, high-quality, affordable care closer to patients' homes. The National Cancer Grid is a key part of this model—the grid is a network of 140 cancer centres, research institutes, patient groups and charitable institutions working in the area of cancer care across India. It has the

mandate of establishing uniform standards of patient care for prevention, diagnosis, and treatment of cancer. These institutes provide specialized training and education in oncology and facilitate collaborative basic, translational and clinical research in cancer.

4. India's hospitals have been identified as case studies in efficiency and frugal innovation. Consider this: At the Tata Memorial Centre, 188 staff treat over 42,000 patients a year; in comparison, at the University of Texas M.D. Anderson Cancer Centre, 1,700 staff treat about the same number of patients in a year. See Bhawna Sirohi et al., 'Developing institutions for cancer care in low-income and middle-income countries: from cancer units to comprehensive cancer centres', *The Lancet Oncology*, Vol. 19, No. 8, 1 August 2018. Available at: https://www.thelancet.com/journals/lanonc/article/PIIS1470-2045(18)30342-5/fulltext

CHAPTER 6: TWICE EXCEPTIONAL

1. 'Cancer Burden in India's North-East States', National Centre for Disease Informatics and Research, 2017. Available at: http://www.ncdirindia.org/All_Reports/Reports_Ne/NE2012_2014/Files/NE_2012_14.pdf

CHAPTER 8: OUT OF REACH

1. 'Report of the Health Survey and Development Committee, Volume Two', Government of India, 1946, pp. 37, 39.

Available at: https://www.nhp.gov.in/sites/default/files/
pdf/Bhore_Committee_Report_Vol2.pdf

2. Meenakshi Gautham and K.M. Shyamprasad, 'The "Basic"
    Doctor for Rural India: A Failed Promise?', *Economic and
    Political Weekly*, Vol. 45, No. 38, 2010. Available at: http://
    www.jstor.org/stable/25742090

3. 'Report of the Health Survey and Development Committee,
    Volume Two', Government of India, 1946, p. 340. Available
    at: https://www.nhp.gov.in/sites/default/files/pdf/Bhore_
    Committee_Report_Vol2.pdf

4. As of 31 December 2017, there were 1,062,398 allopathic
    doctors registered in India. With a population of 1.33 billion,
    this works out to 8 doctors per 10,000 population. Figures
    reported in 'Lok Sabha Unstarred Question No. 1728:
    Shortage of Doctors', Government of India, 27 July 2018.
    Available at: http://164.100.47.190/loksabhaquestions/
    annex/15/AU1728.pdf

    The Medical Council of India (MCI) was, until recently,
    the apex body responsible for establishing and maintaining the
    standards of medical education, and the recognition of qualified
    medical practitioners. Recent legislation has seen it in the
    process of being replaced by a National Medical Commission.
    The MCI's registries are still, however, the primary source for
    data on the number of doctors in the country.

    The data on density of physicians for all other countries
    comes from 'Global Health Observatory', World Health
    Organization, 2017. Available at: https://www.who.int/
    gho/health_workforce/physicians_density/en/

5. Basant Potnuru, 'Aggregate Availability of Doctors in India: 2014-2030', *Indian Journal of Public Health*, Vol. 61, No. 3, 2017. Available at: http://www.ijph.in/article.asp?issn=0019-557X;year=2017;volume=61;issue=3;spage=182;epage=187;aulast=Potnuru;type=0

6. The target levels of doctor and nurse density are based on the norms of ten doctors per 10,000 population and three nurses per doctor, established in 'Report of High-Level Expert Group on Universal Health Coverage', Planning Commission of India, 2011. Available at: http://planningcommission.nic.in/reports/genrep/rep_uhc0812.pdf

7. Mohandas K. Mallath et al., 'The Growing Burden of Cancer in India: Epidemiology and Social Context', *The Lancet Oncology*, Vol. 15, No. 6, April 2014. Available at: https://www.thelancet.com/journals/lanonc/article/PIIS1470-2045(14)70115-9/fulltext?

   Mental health workforce in India (per 100,000 population) includes psychiatrists (0.3), nurses (0.8), psychologists (0.07) and social workers (0.07). 'Mental health workers', World Health Organisation, 2016. Available at: http://apps.who.int/gho/data/view.main.HWF11v

8. Anup Karan et al., 'Size, composition and distribution of human resource for health in India: new estimates using National Sample Survey and Registry data', *BMJ Open*, 2019. Available at: https://protect-eu.mimecast.com/s/97JKCZY8nI88GjjIjWqIS?domain=bmjopen.bmj.com; https://bmjopen.bmj.com/content/bmjopen/9/4/e025979.full.pdf

Notes

CHAPTER 9: IMBALANCES

1. According to 'Indian Public Health Standards (IPHS) for Primary Health Centres (PHCs)', Government of India, 2006, the population coverage norms required from PHCs is one per 20,000 population in hilly areas, and one per 30,000 in plains. Available at: http://www.iapsmgc.org/userfiles/4IPHS_for_PHC.pdf

   A recent government study found that some states in India had far fewer PHCs than recommended, resulting in far poorer coverage ratios. For instance, the state of Jharkhand had one PHC per 84,077 population and Bihar had one PHC per 48,626 population. See 'Rural Health Statistics 2018', Ministry of Health & Family Welfare. Available at: https://nrhm-mis.nic.in/Pages/RHS2018.aspx?RootFolder=%2FRURAL%20HEALTH%20STATISTICS%2F%28A%29%20RHS%20-%202018&FolderCTID=0x01200057278FD1EC909F429B03E86C7A7C3F31&View={09DDD7F4-80D0-42E3-8969-2307C0D97DDB}

2. To get an accurate picture of the reality on the ground, we culled information from a variety of sources. These include: 'Rural Health Statistics 2017', Government of India. Available at: https://data.gov.in/catalog/rural-health-statistics-2017; Sumitra Debroy, 'Rural Areas Face Shortage of Essential Drugs: Survey', *The Times of India,* 14 April 2011. Available at: https://timesofindia.indiatimes.com/city/mumbai/Rural-areas-face-shortage-of-essential-drugs-Survey/articleshow/7976627.cms; and Afshan Yasmeen, 'Only One

Doctor in Most Primary Health Centres', *The Hindu*, 1 April 2018. Available at: https://www.thehindu.com/news/national/only-one-doctor-in-most-primary-health-centres/article23408696.ece

On average, 40 per cent of doctors and healthcare providers are absent from work on a typical day. Karthik Muralidharan et al., 'Is there a Doctor in the House? Medical Worker Absence in India', *Scholars at Harvard*, 12 April 2011. Available at: https://scholar.harvard.edu/files/kremer/files/is_there_a_doctor_in_the_house_-_12_april_2011.pdf

3. Jishnu Das et al., 'Quality and Accountability in Health Care Delivery: Audit-Study Evidence from Primary Care in India', *American Economic Review*, Vol. 106, No. 12, 2016. Available at: https://www.nber.org/papers/w21405.pdf

4. The numbers across nineteen states are estimated at between 50 and 80 per cent. Karthik Muralidharan et al., 'Medical Advice Quality and Availability in Rural India', The World Bank, 15 April 2015. Available at: http://pubdocs.worldbank.org/en/161151429125257286/13-Medical-Advice-Quality-and-Availability-in-Rural-India-MAQARI-Karthik-Muralidharan

5. Haidar Naqvi, 'Unnao Quack, Accused of Infecting 58 People with HIV by Using Same Syringe, Arrested', *Hindustan Times*, 7 February 2018. Available at: https://www.hindustantimes.com/india-news/unnao-quack-accused-of-infecting-58-with-hiv-by-using-single-syringe-arrested/story-UA5D7m3Amihmax1LI6b4iP.html

6. 'Medical Tourism in India to Touch US$8 Billion by 2020', Grant Thornton, 31 October 2015. Available at https://

www.grantthornton.in/news-centre/medical-tourism-in-india-to-touch-us$-8-billion-by-2020-grant-thornton/

7. The epidemiological transition is described in detail in 'India: Health of the Nation's States', Indian Council of Medical Research, Public Health Foundation of India, and Institute for Health Metrics and Evaluation, 2017. Available at: https://www.healthdata.org/sites/default/files/files/policy_report/2017/India_Health_of_the_Nation%27s_States_Report_2017.pdf

CHAPTER 10: OUTREACH

1. 'About Pradhan Mantri Jan Arogya Yojana (PM-JAY)', National Health Authority. Available at https://www.pmjay.gov.in/about-pmjay

CHAPTER 11: BRIDGING ACCESS

1. Learning outcomes: 'Annual Status of Education Report (ASER) 2018', ASER Centre, 2018. Available at: http://img.asercentre.org/docs/ASER%202018/Release%20Material/aser2018nationalfindings.pdf; ASER 2018 covered 596 districts in rural India and surveyed a total of 354,944 households and 546,527 children in the age group three to sixteen.

    Enrolment rates: 'Educational Statistics At A Glance', Ministry of Human Resource Development, Department of School Education & Literacy, Statistics Division, New Delhi, 2018. Available at: https://mhrd.gov.in/sites/upload_files/mhrd/files/statistics-new/ESAG-2018.pdf

2. Sumant Banerji, 'The Case of the Vanishing Drivers', *Business Today*, 22 May 2016. Available at: https://www.businesstoday.in/magazine/features/road-transport-decline-due-to-high-demand-for-truck-drivers/story/232028.html

3. On pending cases: '3.3 crore cases pending in Indian courts, pendency figure at its highest: CJI Dipak Misra', *Business Today*, 28 June 2018. Available at: https://www.businesstoday.in/current/economy-politics/3-3-crore-cases-pending-indian-courts-pendency-figure-highest-cji-dipak-misra/story/279664.html

   On vacancies: Vishnu Padmanabhan and Sriharsha Devulapalli, 'India's next generation reforms must begin in courts', *Mint*, 18 June 2019. Available at: https://www.livemint.com/news/india/india-s-next-generation-reforms-must-begin-in-courts-1560838699823.html

   On use of judges' time and the duration of resolution: 'Time-and-Motion Study of Four District and Sessions Courts in Bangalore, Karnataka', DAKSH, November 2016; Siddharth Mandrekar Rao, 'Another New Tool For An Age Old Problem?', DAKSH, 2018. Available at: http://dakshindia.org/another-new-tool-for-an-age-old-problem/; 'India's judge-population ratio goes up marginally', *The Economic Times*, 7 January 2018. Available at: https://economictimes.indiatimes.com/news/politics-and-nation/indias-judge-population-ratio-goes-up-marginally/articleshow/62400461.cms

   India's ranking on Ease of Doing Business 2019 (on the metric of 'enforcing contracts'): 'Doing Business 2019',

World Bank, 31 October 2018. Available at: https://www.doingbusiness.org/content/dam/doingBusiness/media/Annual-Reports/English/DB2019-report_web-version.pdf

CHAPTER 12: AN UNLIKELY OFFICER

1. Bathinda is a city in the southern part of the Indian state of Punjab.
2. Dowry refers to the parental transfer of monetary gifts, goods or property to their child's married family at the time of the wedding.

CHAPTER 13: THE TALENT DIVIDEND

1. 'Why India needs women to work', *The Economist*, 5 July 2018. Available at: https://www.economist.com/leaders/2018/07/05/why-india-needs-women-to-work
2. PLFS 2017–18.
3. Estimates on the proportion of the workforce educated to secondary level and above is based on analysis by Tata Sons, using data from past national employment surveys. These include PLFS 2017–18 and the 55th round (1999–2000) of the National Sample Survey Organisation's 'Employment and Unemployment in India' report. The share of the workforce—both men and women—educated to secondary level or above, rose by 14 percentage points over the eighteen years from 1999 to 2017. That works out to around 12 percentage points over fifteen years.

Notes

The estimated GDP impact is based on analysis by Tata Sons and Dalberg. It is a supply-side analysis of the GDP increment if half (~60 million) of the secondary and above educated women out of the workforce (~120 million) join paid work. The increment is based on the increase in the number of workers (₹25 trillion or $350 billion) and the accompanying productivity boost that these women bring to the economy given their educational profile (₹6 trillion or $90 billion). Using the references below, the higher education profile translates to a 25 per cent improvement in productivity over the average Indian worker. Note that the estimations are subject to the ability to find appropriate jobs given labour market constraints and the pace at which such absorption can take place.

Angel de la Fuente and Rafael Domenech, 'Human Capital in Growth Regressions: How much Difference Does Data Quality Make?', OECD Economics Department Working Papers, 2000. Available at: https://econpapers.repec.org/paper/oececoaaa/262-en.htm; Barbara Sianesi and John Van Reenen, 'The Returns to Education: Macroeconomics', *Journal of Economic Surveys*, Vol. 17, No. 2, 2003. Available at: https://onlinelibrary.wiley.com/doi/abs/10.1111/1467-6419.00192

4. Career Aspirations: 'Teen Age Girls Survey (TAG Survey)', Naandi Foundation, 2018. Available at: https://www.nanhikali.org/teenagegirlsurvey/TAG-Report.pdf

   Potential workforce participation for women: Erin K. Fletcher et al., 'Women and Work in India: Descriptive Evidence and a Review of Potential Policies', HKS Faculty

Notes

Research Working Paper Series RWP18-004, December 2017. Available at: https://www.hks.harvard.edu/sites/default/files/centers/cid/files/publications/faculty-working-papers/women_work_india_cidwp339.pdf

5. On the G20 comparison: 'Why India needs women to work', *The Economist,* 5 July 2018. Available at: https://www.economist.com/leaders/2018/07/05/why-india-needs-women-to-work

    Other comparisons: Analysis by Tata Sons using PLFS 2017–18 and the ILOSTAT database.

6. Explaining the decline: K.P. Kannan and G. Raveendran, 'Counting and Profiling the Missing Labour Force', *Economic and Political Weekly*, Vol. XLVII, No. 6, 11 February 2012. Available at: https://www.epw.in/journal/2012/06/discussion/counting-and-profiling-missing-labour-force.html

    Job loss due to mechanization: 'Culture and the labour market keep India's women at home', *The Economist,* 5 July 2018. Available at: https://www.economist.com/briefing/2018/07/05/culture-and-the-labour-market-keep-indias-women-at-home

    CMIE estimates: Mahesh Vyas, '11 million jobs lost in 2018', Centre for Monitoring Indian Economy Pvt. Ltd., 08 January 2019. Available at: https://www.cmie.com/kommon/bin/sr.php?kall=warticle&dt=2019-01-08%2009:28:37&msec=666

7. Economic importance of women's work participation: 'A guide to womenomics', *The Economist,* 12 April 2006. Available at: https://www.economist.com/finance-and-economics/2006/04/12/a-guide-to-womenomics

Female to male ratios in managerial positions: Berta Esteve-Volart, 'Gender Discrimination and Growth: Theory and Evidence from India', STICERD - Development Economics Papers, LSE, 2004. Available at: https://EconPapers.repec.org/RePEc:cep:stidep:42

CHAPTER 15: TWICE-HIT ECONOMY

1. Luis Alberto Andres et al., 'Precarious Drop Reassessing Patterns of Female Labor Force Participation in India', World Bank, April 2017. Available at: http://documents.worldbank.org/curated/en/559511491319990632/pdf/WPS8024.pdf
2. In many countries, the M-curve has transformed into a trapezoid shape largely due to policy interventions. Take the case of Japan. While it displayed an M-curve until a few years ago, the curve is flattening—signifying that the dip that typically tends to happen at the juncture of marriage/childbirth is not taking place. This has been attributed to policy decisions concerning more day-care support, parental leave benefits, rise in part-time employment, and disclosure of diversity-related data by organizations, among others. For more details see Kathy Matsui et al, 'Womenomics 5.0', Goldman Sachs, 18 April 2019. Available at: https://www.goldmansachs.com/insights/pages/womenomics-5.0/multimedia/womenomics-5.0-report.pdf; Hikariko Yazaki and Miho Gatayama, 'Japan's female labor force set to toss out M-curve', *Nikkei Asian Review*, 17 September 2017. Available at: https://asia.nikkei.com/Politics/Japan-s-female-labor-force-set-to-toss-out-M-curve

3. As much as 31 per cent of girls and women between the ages of fifteen and forty-nine years have given birth before the age of twenty; National Family Health Survey (NFHS-4), Ministry of Health and Family Welfare, 2015-16. Available at: http://rchiips.org/nfhs/NFHS-4Reports/India.pdf

4. Unpaid care work: 'The Power of Parity: How Advancing Women's Equality Can Add $12 Trillion To Global Growth', McKinsey Global Institute, September 2015. Available at: https://www.mckinsey.com/~/media/McKinsey/Featured%20Insights/Employment%20and%20Growth/How%20advancing%20womens%20equality%20can%20add%2012%20trillion%20to%20global%20growth/MGI%20Power%20of%20parity_Full%20report_September%202015.ashx

   Value of unpaid care work: 'The Power of Parity: Advancing Women's Equality In India', McKinsey Global Institute, November 2015. Available at: https://www.mckinsey.com/~/media/McKinsey/Featured%20Insights/Employment%20and%20Growth/The%20power%20of%20parity%20Advancing%20womens%20equality%20in%20India/MGI%20India%20parity_Full%20report_November%202015.ashx

5. Additional cost for safety: Girija Borker, 'Safety First: Perceived Risk of Street Harassment and Educational Choices of Women', Indian Statistical Institute, 2018. Available at: https://www.isid.ac.in/~epu/acegd2018/papers/GirijaBorker.pdf

   Hesitation on migration: Rohini Pande et al., 'How To Get India's Women Working? First, Let Them Out of the House', *IndiaSpend*, 9 April 2016. Available at: https://

archive.indiaspend.com/cover-story/how-to-get-indias-women-working-first-let-them-out-of-the-house-74364

6. Assumptions for the chart are as follows: (i) The base salary is the indicative salary of a salaried male undergraduate (from PLFS 2017–18); (ii) a wage penalty of 17 per cent is deducted based on the wage differential between men and women (from PLFS 2017–18), to arrive at the effective salary for a working woman; (iii) based on market rates, estimates for childcare, additional women's personal care products (likened to 'pink tax'), and safer commute options have been deducted to arrive at net salary.

7. According to the Census 2011, the child sex ratio (0-6 years) has shown a decline from 927 females per thousand males in 2001 to 919 females per thousand males in 2011, although the overall sex ratio has improved.

8. 'Indian Human Development Survey', University of Maryland and the National Council of Applied Economic Research, 2011–2012. Available at: https://ihds.umd.edu//

CHAPTER 17: RELEASING THE TALENT GRIDLOCK

1. ILOSTAT database (women 15+). For details on 25–54 years, see: https://www.brookings.edu/blog/up-front/2019/03/26/women-staging-a-labor-force-comeback/

2. Anne Brink et al., 'Maximum Fee vs. Child Benefit: A Welfare Analysis of Swedish Child-Care Fee Reform', The Institute for the Study of Labor, April 2007. Available at: http://ftp.iza.org/dp2748.pdf; Bettina Siflinger and Gerard van den Berg, 'The Effects of a Universal Child Care Reform on

Child Health–Evidence from Sweden', Annual Conference 2016 (Augsburg): Demographic Change 145765, Verein für Socialpolitik/German Economic Association, 2016. Available at: https://ideas.repec.org/p/zbw/vfsc16/145765.html

3. Mexico's childcare model: 'Children's Stay Program to Support Working Mothers', *Gobierno de México*. Available at: https://www.gob.mx/bienestar/acciones-y-programas/estancias-infantiles-para-apoyar-a-madres-trabajadoras

    Outcomes of Mexico's childcare model: Emma Samman et al., 'Women's work: Mothers, children and the global childcare crisis', Overseas Development Institute, March 2016. Available at: https://www.odi.org/sites/odi.org.uk/files/odi-assets/publications-opinion-files/10333.pdf

4. On Mobile Creches: 'Our Story', Mobile Creches. Available at: https://www.mobilecreches.org/our-story

    On the impact of Mobile Creches: Annabelle Timsit, 'An Indian nonprofit is showing how free childcare at work can help disrupt the poverty cycle', *Quartz India,* 30 January 2019. Available at: https://qz.com/india/1532477/the-impact-of-free-childcare-on-indias-poverty-cycle/; Annual Report 2017–18, Mobile Creches. Available at: https://docs.wixstatic.com/ugd/57f05d_c7fab2321a934c85b19af98383bd1158.pdf

5. Balwadis are full-day community day-care centres operated by the NGO Seva Mandir in the villages of Rajasthan, initially started to plug the gaps where Anganwadi centres (public day-care centres) didn't exist. According to impact reports, Balwadis have enabled more than half of enrolled children's mothers to pursue livelihood activities.

6. 'Tackling Childcare: The Business Case for Employer Supported Childcare', International Finance Corporation, 2017. Available at: https://www.ifc.org/wps/wcm/connect/cd79e230-3ee2-46ae-adc5-e54d3d649f31/01817+WB+Childcare+Report_FinalWeb3.pdf?MOD=AJPERES&CVID=lXu9vP-

7. James Heckman, 'Invest in Early Childhood Development: Reduce Deficits, Strengthen the Economy', Heckman: The economics of human potential. Available at: https://heckmanequation.org/resource/invest-in-early-childhood-development-reduce-deficits-strengthen-the-economy/

8. Market estimation: Tata Sons and Dalberg analysis.

   Employment potential in the childcare industry: Tata Sons analysis; Somatish Banerji et al., 'By Women – For Women, Building the childcare ecosystem in India', Intellecap, 10 December 2018. Available at: https://www.intellecap.com/wp-content/uploads/2018/12/By-Women-for-Women_Building-the-childcare-ecosystem-in-India.pdf

9. Megha Singh and Neelima Mishra, 'Felt Obligation and Ageing: A Socio-Cultural Issue', *International Research Journal of Arts and Social Sciences (ISSN: 2251-0028)*, Vol. 1(1), pp. 1–7, September 2012. Available at: https://www.interesjournals.org/articles/felt-obligation-and-ageing-a-sociocultural-issue.pdf

10. Elder care in Japan: Chris Farrell, 'What Japan can teach us about long-term care', *Forbes*, 24 August 2015. Available at: https://www.forbes.com/sites/nextavenue/2015/08/24/what-japan-can-teach-us-about-long-term-care/#424f8ab6705d; Nanako Tamiya et al., 'Population ageing and well-being: lessons from Japan's long-term care insurance policy', *The Lancet*, 30 August

2011. Available at: https://www.thelancet.com/journals/lancet/article/PIIS0140-6736(11)61176-8/fulltext

Karnataka's Grama Hiriyara Kendras: These village senior care centres started in 2015 in three villages of Anekal Taluk. The centres are anchored by the Senior Citizen Health Service wing of St. John's National Academy of Health Sciences. Available at: http://www.stjohns.in/Special_services/Senior CitizensProgramme

11. Section 66(1)(b) of the Factories Act, 1948 states that no woman shall be required or allowed to work in any factory except between the hours of 6 a.m. and 7 p.m.; Section 25 of the Beedi and Cigar Workers (Conditions of Employment) Act, 1966 stipulates that no woman shall be required or allowed to work in any industrial premise except between 6 a.m. and 7 p.m.; Section 46(1)(b) of the Mines Act, 1952 prohibits employment of women in any mine above ground except between the hours of 6 a.m. and 7 p.m. Available at: https://labour.gov.in/womenlabour/about-women-labour

12. Jagriti Chandra and Sumant Sen, 'Only 20% of Nirbhaya Fund has been used by States until 2018', *The Hindu*, 30 June 2019. Available at: https://www.thehindu.com/news/national/only-20-of-nirbhaya-fund-has-been-used-by-states-until-2018/article28230097.ece

13. 'Maternity and paternity at work: Law and practice across the world', International Labour Organization, 2014. Available at: https://www.ilo.org/wcmsp5/groups/public/---dgreports/---dcomm/---publ/documents/publication/wcms_242615.pdf

14. Canadian employment law currently allows for elder-care leave. In 2018, Singapore policymakers began debating a similar legislation.

15. '14th International Review of Leave Policies and Related Research 2018', International Network On Leave Policies And Research, September 2018. Available at: https://www.leavenetwork.org/fileadmin/user_upload/k_leavenetwork/annual_reviews/Leave_Review_2018.pdf; Elly-Ann Johansson, 'The effect of own and spousal parental leave on earnings', Institute for Labour Market Policy Evaluation, 2010. Available at: https://www.ifau.se/globalassets/pdf/se/2010/wp10-4-the-effect-of-own-and-spousal-parental-leave-on-earnings.pdf

16. Gender Pay Gap Service, UK Government. Available at: https://gender-pay-gap.service.gov.uk/viewing/search-results?t=1&search=

17. On Breakthrough: 'About Breakthrough', Breakthrough. Available at: https://inbreakthrough.org/our-story/

    Outcomes for girls: 'Changing Gender Norms', Breakthrough and J-PAL, 2018. Available at: https://docs.google.com/viewerng/viewer?url=https://inbreakthrough.org/wp-content/uploads/2018/11/jpal-1.pdf

    Outcomes for boys: Diva Dhar et al., 'Reshaping Adolescents' Gender Attitudes: Evidence from a School-Based Experiment in India', NBER Working Paper No. 25331, 30 November 2018. Available at: https://www.nber.org/papers/w25331.pdf

18. Tata STRIVE is a pan-India programme that focuses on skilling India's youth for employment, entrepreneurship

and community enterprise. The core philosophy is to create vocational courses that develop skilled talent across the entire industrial spectrum, as well as nurturing entrepreneurial ambition. Available at: https://www.tatastrive.com/

19. M.L. Melly Maitreyi, 'Women at the wheel drive change', *The Hindu*, 7 March 2018. Available at: https://www.thehindu. com/news/cities/Hyderabad/women-at-the-wheel-drive-change/article22953660.ece

20. Analysis using data from PLFS 2017–18. Formal workers are regular/salaried workers, and informal workers include self-employed and casual workers.

21. 'The Power of Parity: Advancing Women's Equality in Asia Pacific', McKinsey Global Institute, April 2018. Available at: https://www..mckinsey.com/~/media/McKinsey/ Featured%20Insights/Gender%20Equality/The%20power%20 of%20parity%20Advancing%20womens%20equality%20 in%20Asia%20Pacific/MGI-The-power-of-parity-Advancing-womens-equality-in-Asia-pacific-Full-report.ashx; 'Women-owned SMEs in Indonesia: A Golden Opportunity for Local Financial Institutions', International Finance Corporation (in partnership with USAID), March 2016. Available at: https://www.ifc.org/wps/wcm/connect/260f2097-e440-4599-91ec-e42d45cf3913/SME+Indonesia+Final_ Eng.pdf?MOD=AJPERES&CVID=lj8qhPY; and 'Sixth Economic Census', Ministry of Statistics and Programme Implementation, 2013-14. Available at: http://www.mospi. gov.in/sites/default/files/economic-census/sixth_economic_ census/all_india/11_ChapterVI_6ecRep_0.pdf

CHAPTER 18: THE EASIEST FIX

1. Anup Karan et al., 'Size, composition and distribution of human resource for health in India: new estimates using National Sample Survey and Registry data', *BMJ Open*, 2019. Available at: https://bmjopen.bmj.com/content/bmjopen/9/4/e025979.full.pdf

CHAPTER 20: JOBS COUNT

1. All figures sourced from 'World Population Prospects – 2017 Revision', UN DESA. Available at: https://www.un.org/development/desa/publications/graphic/wpp2017-global-population. The medium fertility variant was used for calculation of age-group-wise projections. For India, UN population growth rates were applied to the 2011 census population.

There are multiple definitions of working-age population. India has typically considered fifteen- to fifty-nine-year-olds to be of working age, since the official retirement age for government employees was sixty for a long time. Increasingly however, international organizations and national statistical bodies are adopting a convention of reporting figures for a working-age definition of fifteen years and above. This is both a matter of convenience—dropping the upper end solves the challenge of different retirement ages in different countries—and a reflection of trends in the labour market. This is especially the case in developing countries like India, with large informal workforces, where many people do not earn and save enough to retire at a certain age. They may continue working well past sixty or sixty-five, in the absence of a retirement fund or monetizable assets to depend on. We adopt this convention unless explicitly indicated otherwise.

2. Mihir Sharma, 'India's Youth are the World's Future', *Bloomberg*, 8 September 2017. Available at: https://www.bloomberg.com/opinion/articles/2017-09-08/india-s-youth-are-the-world-s-future

3. The 'labour force' includes both people who are working ('workforce') and who are looking for work, or say they would work if given the opportunity ('unemployed'). The unemployment rate is expressed as a percentage of the labour force.

4. Estimates for the population in the age group of fifteen years and older, as of 2017, developed independently by Tata Sons. The estimates are developed using decadal growth rates from the Census of India 2001 and 2011, at the level of sex (male, female), age group (0–14, 15–59 and 60+), and location (urban, rural). Data on the unemployment rate is from PLFS 2017–18.

5. Technically, the share of the working-age population that is working or looking for work is called the labour force participation rate (LFPR). Headline figures such as the unemployment rate and the labour force participation rate in India are sourced from PLFS 2017–18. Figures in millions are estimates by Tata Sons, developed by combining the headline figures (in percentage terms) with estimates of population, separately projected from the Census of India 2001 and 2011.

Labour force participation rate for China is a CEIC estimate, based on World Bank data. Available at: https://www.ceicdata.com/en/indicator/china/labour-force-participation-rate. China's LFPR estimate pertains to the age group fifteen and above.

6. We refer to those with more than a secondary level of education as 'educated'. They may have graduate degrees, postgraduate degrees or shorter two-year diplomas. All figures from PLFS 2017–18.

7. There are two concepts involved in defining informality. One can look at the company—its size, whether it is registered with the government, pays taxes and is liable to provide certain protections to workers. Firms that fulfil these criteria are called 'organized'. Firms that do not—that are too small, and fall below legal thresholds for registration or worker protections—are 'unorganized'.

    One can also consider the characteristics of the job itself—whether there is a contract, whether one is assured work and payment (either indefinitely, or for some defined number of days), and the ease with which one can be fired. Jobs may be classified into formal (a contract ensures a certain period of guaranteed employment, with protections against summary dismissal); informal (there may or may not be a contract, but duration and payment are assured in some form); or casual (there is neither contract nor assurance of work from one day to the next.)

    In this book, we use the terms 'informal economy', 'informal sector', and 'informal work' in a less technical or precise sense. We mean it as shorthand for everyone who is not either a full-time employee or a contract worker at an organized firm. In other words, informal workers fall somewhere on the spectrum that runs from a self-employed or casual labourer at one end, to full-time workers—with or without contracts—at unorganized micro and small firms at the other end. The concept of formality/informality does not translate easily to the agricultural sector, in part because it relates to whether one works for a registered factory or company, whereas there is no such thing as an unregistered farm. Still, if we define formality in terms of job security, regular income, contracts for labour, or non-wage/social security benefits, the farm workforce would be considered informal.

8. A beedi is a thin mini-cigar filled with tobacco flakes.

9. Labour productivity (which we refer to as 'productivity' throughout this book) refers to the quantity of goods and services a worker produces in an hour of work. How much a worker earns—their wage—is, all else being equal, determined by the value of goods and services they are producing per hour—their productivity. Thus, when comparing industries/sectors of the economy, we use average wage levels as a proxy for productivity, recognizing certain shortcomings—for example, the structure of different sectors, such as the strength of labour unions or how heavy automation adoption is, also affects the wage–productivity relationship. Broadly, it is assumed that a sector with higher wages is more productive than one with lower wage levels.

10. Differences in daily earnings are based on data from PLFS 2017–18. Informal sector workers include casual and self-employed workers. The former earns on average 55–70 per cent less than formal sector workers, while the latter earns 25–30 per cent less per day of work. In aggregate, the differential between the formal and informal sectors is 30–40 per cent. The average wage per month for all formal sector workers is ₹16,500 ($236) while it is ₹10,600 ($152) for informal sector workers.

CHAPTER 22: A TWO-TRACK ECONOMY

1. Primary education includes all levels of educational achievement below tenth grade. Secondary education includes those who have completed tenth or twelfth grade. Tertiary education includes those with graduate and postgraduate degrees, which typically involve three to four years (or more) of study at a university after the completion of a secondary education. We also consider those completing shorter diploma courses—that typically take one to two years, after secondary education—as tertiary educated. Nearly 64 per cent of India's working-age population (fifteen years and above) has an educational attainment, at best, up to primary school. This includes around 27 per cent of the working-age population that is not literate. This figure is even higher in the workforce, with nearly 67 per cent having, at best, a primary education. Data based on PLFS 2017–18.

    Vocational and skills training offers an alternative set of qualifications to those unable to complete formal secondary or tertiary education. It usually involves undertaking a two- to three-month course, at a recognized government or private institution, in order to gain skills for a particular type of job. The PLFS 2017–18 estimates that only 2 per cent of those in the age group 15–59 and 2.5 per cent in the age group 15–29 have received formal vocational training. Non-formal training—such as learning on-the-job, self-learning or being taught by parents—is much more prevalent, with 6 per cent in the age group of 15–59 years reportedly receiving non-formal training. The figures are similar to those in the last large sample survey conducted by the National Sample Survey Organisation—it found that 2.2 per cent in the age group of 15–59 years received formal vocational training, with 8.6 per cent reporting non-formal vocational training.

2. Rajya Sabha Unstarred Question No. 1224, answered by the Ministry of Skill Development and Entrepreneurship on 13 February 2019. Available at: https://164.100.158.235/question/annex/248/Au1224.pdf

For a discussion on the challenges with skilling, see: Antara Sengupta, 'India's skilling challenge: Lessons from UK, Germany's vocational training models', Observer Research Foundation, 4 June 2018. Available at: https://www.orfonline.org/expert-speak/indias-skilling-challenge-lessons-from-uk-germanys-vocational-training-models/

Haris Zarigar, 'Lack of quality trainers impending India's skill mission', Mint, 19 February 2018. Available at: https://www.livemint.com/Industry/iLeYEW1rqsxkIS3DA7FIeN/Lack-of-quality-trainers-impending-Indias-skill-mission.html

3. Analysis by Tata Sons based on multiple sources.

    Employment levels and share of secondary educated workers in different sectors for 2011 is based on unit-level data from the sixty-eighth round of the National Sample Survey Organisation's Employment and Unemployment Survey, 2011–12.

    Real Gross Value Added (GVA) from the National Accounts Statistics (NAS) 2011–12, Central Statistics Office, Ministry of Statistics and Programme Implementation.

    Split of GVA between organized and unorganized manufacturing from Radhicka Kapoor, 'Understanding the Performance of India's Manufacturing Sector: Evidence from Firm Level Data', Centre for Sustainable Employment Working Paper 2018-2, March 2018.

4. '2018 Talent Shortage Survey: Solving the Talent Shortage', Manpower Group, 2018. Available at: https://www. manpowergroup.co.in/TalentShortageSurveyIndia2018.pdf

    Judges' numbers: Pradeep Thakur, 'Govt plans exam to recruit 6,000 judges for lower courts', *The Times of India,* 22 October 2018. Available at: https://timesofindia. indiatimes.com/india/govt-plans-exam-to-recruit-6000-judges-for-lower-courts/articleshow/66309316.cms

    Physicians' numbers: 'Lok Sabha Unstarred Question No. 1728,' Ministry of Health and Family Welfare, July 2018. Available at: http://164.100.47.190/loksabhaquestions/annex/15/AU1728.pdf

    Elementary school teacher numbers: 'How have States Designed their School Education Budgets?', Centre for Budget and Accountability (CBGA) and Child Rights and

You (CRY), 2016. Available at: https://www.cry.org/ resources/pdf/Study%20Report%20by%20CBGA%20 and%20CRY-1.PDF

Private sector vacancy numbers: '2018 Talent Shortage Survey', Manpower Group. Available at: https://insights. manpowergroupsolutions.com/2018-talent-shortage-survey/

5. Reproduced from Ajit K. Ghose's 'India Employment Report 2016', Institute for Human Development. US data taken from 'Current Population Survey, 2012 Annual Social and Economic Supplement', U.S. Census Bureau, 2012. The grouping 'Primary and below' includes not literate and those educated up to the eighth grade (that is, both primary and middle school).

6. UP messengers' job application numbers: Pathikrit Chakraborty, 'In UP, 3,700 PhD holders apply for messenger's jobs', *The Times of India,* 30 August 2018. Available at: https:// timesofindia.indiatimes.com/city/lucknow/3700-phd-holders-apply-for-messengers-job/articleshow/65601510.cms

7. Calculated using data tables on 'Enrolment by Level of Education' and 'Expenditure on Education (Government) in PPP$', downloaded from UNESCO Institute for Statistics.

8. Nancy Birdsall et al. (edited by Lawrence MacDonald), 'The East Asian miracle: Economic growth and public policy: Main report (English)', World Bank, 2013. Available at: http://documents.worldbank.org/curated/ en/975081468244550798/Main-report

The link between secondary-educated workers and economic growth is discussed in Robert J. Barro, 'Education and Economic Growth', OECD, 2001. Available at: https://

www.oecd.org/education/innovation-education/1825455.
pdf; and T.R. Breton, 'The role of education in economic
growth: theory, history and current returns', *Educational
Research*, Vol. 55, No. 2, pp. 121–138, 2013. Available at:
https://www.tandfonline.com/doi/abs/10.1080/00131881.
2013.801241

CHAPTER 23: TWICE EXPOSED

1. The monthly income of an average Indian is nearly ₹11,900,
    which translates to ₹142,800 ($2,040) per year (India's per
    capita income) at an exchange rate of ₹70 per US $. Rajappa's
    earning of ₹20,000 per month is just over two-thirds higher
    than this.

CHAPTER 24: ESCALATOR SECTORS

1. 'South Asia Economic Focus, Spring 2018: Jobless
    Growth?', World Bank, 15 April 2018. Available at:
    https://openknowledge.worldbank.org/bitstream/
    handle/10986/29650/9781464812842.pdf?
2. Analysis for India based on the data release accompanying the
    publication: D.K. Das et al., 'Measuring Productivity at the
    Industry Level–The India KLEMS Database', Reserve Bank
    of India, March 2018. Available at: https://m.rbi.org.in/
    Scripts/PublicationReportDetails.aspx?UrlPage=&ID=894

    Korea data from the World KLEMS Initiative, who in
    turn source it from the Korea Productivity Centre.

3. Employment shares from PLFS 2017–18. Contribution to GDP reflects the sectoral shares in nominal gross value-added, as sourced from CEIC. Data for 2017 is used for comparability with employment data from 2017.

CHAPTER 27: THE ENTREPRENEUR'S TALE

1. Kirana stores are neighbourhood mom-and-pop grocery retail stores in India.
2. Rajasthan is a state in western India, with a population of roughly 70 million.

CHAPTER 29: THE GREAT SKEW

1. SME definition: There are different ways of classifying enterprises—based on revenue, capital investment, turnover or number of workers, among other considerations. The Indian Ministry of Micro, Small and Medium Enterprises (MSME) uses a definition based on investment. However, given that the focus of this book is jobs, we have generally used an employment-based definition for our purpose. Globally, the most widely used definitions categorize micro enterprises as those hiring less than ten people; small as between ten and forty-nine; and medium as between fifty and 249. Self-employed individuals (that is, those who have no additional employees) are also considered micro enterprises. Wherever possible, we have used this definition, unless otherwise specified in the endnotes.

2. Average firm size in India as of 2014 was 2.24. See 'All India Report of Sixth Economic Census', Central Statistics Office, Ministry of Statistics and Programme Implementation, 2014. Available at: http://www.mospi.gov.in/all-india-report-sixth-economic-census

   The Economic Census has well-documented issues in accurately capturing the total number of people employed in firms. See for instance, R. Krishnaswamy and S.L. Shetty, 'Sixth Economic Census 2013: Intriguing Numbers', *Economic & Political Weekly*, Vol. 49, No. 38, 20 September 2014. However, it is the only source that attempts to profile the full spectrum of enterprises in the country. We use elements of the survey, such as the average firm size and the distribution of workers across firms of different sizes. We then apply this data to figures of the overall workforce used in other parts of the book.

   In India, as of 2014, around 174 million people—38 per cent of the workforce—were employed in firms. This number does not include farm workers, public administration and defence employees, or casual labourers. However, it does include employees of government-run enterprises (Public Sector Undertakings or PSUs).

3. Apparel sector size: 'Textiles & Apparel Sector', Department of Industrial Policy and Promotion, 2016. Available at: http://pibphoto.nic.in/documents/rlink/2016/nov/p2016112503.pdf

   Employment in apparel sector in India and China: 'Enterprises in Asia: Fostering Dynamism in SME', Asian Development Bank, 2009. Available at: https://www.adb.

org/sites/default/files/publication/27727/ki2009-special-chapter.pdf

4. Data limitations prevent a direct comparison of like-for-like firm size aligned to the SME definitions (1–9, 10–49, 50–249) we have adopted.

Micro enterprises have low productivity and low prospects of growth: Rana Hasan and Karl Robert L. Jandoc, 'Labor Regulations and the Firm Size Distribution in Indian Manufacturing', Columbia University, 2012. Available at: https://academiccommons.columbia.edu/doi/10.7916/D88G8TVH/

Four-times productivity differential: 'Enterprises in Asia: Fostering Dynamism in SMEs', Asian Development Bank, 2009. Available at: https://www.adb.org/sites/default/files/publication/27727/ki2009-special-chapter.pdf

Eight times as productive: Radhicka Kapoor, 'Creating Jobs in India's Organised Manufacturing Sector', ICRIER Working Paper 286, September 2014. Available at: http://icrier.org/pdf/Working_Paper_286.pdf

5. India's firm size brackets (1–9, 10–199, 200+) are different from the US, Germany, Brazil and Israel (1–9, 10–249, 250+). The comparison is not precise, but indicative.

6. 'All India Report of Sixth Economic Census', Central Statistics Office, 2014

Paan, or betel leaf, is an after-meal digestive, popular in the Indian subcontinent. Paan shops, typically small single-manned roadside outlets, sell rolled paan with slaked lime, betel nut and other flavours.

7. 'The Global Unicorn Club', *CB Insights*, 2019. Accessed on 31 July 2019. Available at: https://www.cbinsights.com/research-unicorn-companies

    Start-up job figures: 'Indian Tech Startup Ecosystem: Approaching Escape Velocity', *NASSCOM* and *Zinnov*, 2018. Available behind paywall at: https://www.nasscom.in/knowledge-center/publications/indian-tech-start-ecosystem-2018-approaching-escape-velocity

    Nearly 121 million people employed in micro firms: Based on analysis by Tata Sons.

CHAPTER 30: GOLDILOCKS ENTREPRENEURS

1. 'Financing India's MSMEs', International Finance Corporation, 2018. Available at: https://www.ifc.org/wps/wcm/connect/dcf9d09d-68ad-4e54-b9b7-614c143735fb/Financing+India%E2%80%99s+MSMEs+-+Estimation+of+Debt+Requirement+of+MSMEs+in+India.pdf?MOD=AJPERES

    Non-banking financial companies (NBFCs) lend and make investments in a similar manner to banks. However, there are a few key differences: 1) NBFCs cannot accept demand deposits; 2) An NBFC is not part of the payment and settlement system and cannot issue cheques drawn on itself; 3) They do not hold a bank licence.
2. India is working to consolidate existing public sector banks to achieve scale, improve efficiency and promote innovation.

Simultaneously, small local area banks (regional rural banks, urban cooperative banks, etc.) are needed to serve small businesses, especially in parts of the country where larger banks do not enjoy the same reach. These banks face issues like an inadequate capital base, weaker governance levels and low diversification of funds, leading to losses and stressed assets. Better monitoring of these banks can help them provide better services to the customers they are relatively well-placed to reach.

The term 'small bank' is a loose term that refers to local, regional, cooperative and community-focused banks that typically serve local businesses. In India, small banks include regional banks and urban cooperative banks; in Europe, small banks include only cooperative banks; and in the US, small banks include regional and community banks.

Six per cent and fifteen per cent figures: 'Financing India's MSMEs', International Finance Corporation, 2018. Available at: https://www.ifc.org/wps/wcm/connect/dcf9d09d-68ad-4e54-b9b7-614c143735fb/Financing+India%E2%80%99s+MSMEs+-+Estimation+of+Debt+Requirement+of+MSMEs+in+India.pdf?MOD=AJPERES

Cooperative bank branches in Europe: 'Annual Report 2017', European Association of Cooperative Banks, 2017. Available at: http://v3.globalcube.net/clients/eacb/content/medias/publications/annual_reports/final_eacb_annual_report_2017_compressed.pdf

Total bank branches in Europe: 'Banking in Europe', European Banking Federation, 2018. Available at: https://www.ebf.eu/wp-content/uploads/2018/09/Banking-in-Europe-2018-EBF-Facts-and-Figures.pdf

SME loans in USA: Karen Gordon Mills and Brayden McCarthy, 'The State of Small Business Lending', Harvard Business School, July 2014. Available at: https://www.hbs.edu/faculty/Publication%20Files/15-004_09b1bf8b-eb2a-4e63-9c4e-0374f770856f.pdf

3. Micro Units Development and Refinance Agency (MUDRA) was set up by the Government of India in 2015. MUDRA partners with banks, microfinance institutions and other lending institutions at a state or regional level to provide credit to small enterprises. The maximum credit limit is ₹1 million (~$14,000). MUDRA is only a refinancing institution and does not lend directly to micro entrepreneurs or individuals.

4. Goods and Services Tax (GST) is an indirect tax regime in India that came into effect on 1 July 2017. It was introduced to replace the multitude of indirect taxes (state value-added tax, central sales tax, octroi duty, etc.) that varied by state. After the implementation of GST, India shifted to a single indirect tax system of varying rates, applicable on all goods and services produced and sold in the country.

5. This is the maximum number of filings that a larger corporation with multiple businesses and a pan-India footprint may have to make. For a firm like Amit's, the number of filings related to labour regulations would be closer to 10–40.

200 laws: Devashish Mitra, 'How labour regulations affect manufacturing in India', *Mint,* 2018. Available at: https://www.livemint.com/Opinion/53blF1v8tQKSap0crJ9YxL/How-labour-regulations-affect-manufacturing-in-India.html

1,800 possible filings: Manish Sabharwal and Sandeep Agrawal, 'Changing the Indian state from bully to ally', *Mint,* 2018. Available at: https://www.livemint.com/Opinion/M3TMqxxMuDNrswoznJCVaO/Opinion--Changing-the-Indian-state-from-bully-to-ally.html

6. 'India jumps 23 spots to No. 77 on World Bank Ease of Doing Business Index', *India Today,* 2018. Available at: https://www.indiatoday.in/business/story/india-ease-of-doing-business-index-77-position-1379663-2018-10-31

7. High-growth and low-growth state figures: 'Ease of Doing Business', NITI Aayog and IDFC Institute, 2017. Available at: https://niti.gov.in/writereaddata/files/document_publication/EoDB_Single.pdf

   Mumbai and Delhi figures: 'Doing Business', World Bank Group, 2019. Available at: http://www.worldbank.org/content/dam/doingBusiness/media/Annual-Reports/English/DB2019-report_web-version.pdf

   OECD figure: 'Doing Business: Regional Profile OECD High Income', World Bank Group, 2019. Available at: http://www.doingbusiness.org/content/dam/doingBusiness/media/Profiles/Regional/DB2019/OECD-High-Income.pdf

8. Mumbai and Delhi figures: 'Doing Business', World Bank Group, 2019. Available at: http://www.worldbank.org/

content/dam/doingBusiness/media/Annual-Reports/
English/DB2019-report_web-version.pdf

OECD figure: 'Doing Business: Regional Profile OECD
High Income', World Bank Group, 2019. Available at: http://
www.doingbusiness.org/content/dam/doingBusiness/media/
Profiles/Regional/DB2019/OECD-High-Income.pdf

CHAPTER 32: EMBRACING EVERYWHERE ENTREPRENEURSHIP

1. South Korea, Singapore: Shankha Chakraborty et
   al., 'Prosperity of Nations: Does culture matter for
   entrepreneurship?', World Bank, 2015. Available at: https://
   blogs.worldbank.org/developmenttalk/prosperity-nations-
   does-culture-matter-entrepreneurship

   Rwanda: Tik Root, 'Start-Ups For the State', *Foreign Policy,*
   2016. Available at: https://foreignpolicy.com/2016/06/26/
   start-ups-for-the-state-rwanda-entrepreneurship/
2. Sang M. Lee et al., 'Impact of Entrepreneurship Education:
   A Comparative Study of the U.S. and Korea', *International
   Entrepreneurship and Management Journal,* 2005. Available at:
   http://cbafiles.unl.edu/public/cbainternal/researchlibrary/
   Impact%20of%20Entrepreneurship%20Education-%20A%20
   Comparative%20Study%20of%20the%20U0.pdf
3. Manish Sabharwal, 'Problem is wages, not jobs; answer lies
   in formalisation, financialisation', *The Indian Express*, 2018.
   Available at: https://indianexpress.com/article/explained/
   manish-sabharwal-problem-is-wages-not-jobs-minimum-
   salary-unemployment-indian-gdp-5106348/

Notes

4. The statutory programmes include the Employees' Provident Fund and Family Pension Schemes, Labour Welfare Fund and Employee State Insurance, to name a few. The quantification of the 'wedge' this creates (the gap between the cost of an employee to the firm and her take-home pay, not including income tax) is based on the stylized example in 'Economic Survey 2015-16', Ministry of Finance, Government of India, 2016. Available at: https://www.indiabudget.gov.in/budget2016-2017/es2015-16/echapvol1-10.pdf

5. 'Future of Jobs in India–Enterprises and Livelihoods: Volumes 1 and 2', Confederation of Indian Industry, 2017. Available at: https://www.cii.in/PublicationDetail.aspx?enc= afvfGzlF0Fcptetf1p0zirJHzFDI6duqPQJnbIo47bgay SEB9GJ5JAAvheCVVV/qQVAYYae8SGEodntCCz 7nK17rgtBzfL6+x4iqLuy8AYyuA8w/FnZkXLkMC r3RYhmCoYlp566LRg2ZYm8OIY3Iw MdDIyKUQ1FK3bGDZxqrs9IznVBA2 WwJNbDm1nTPh2I2

6. 'Districts', Government of India, 2019. Available at: http://www.goidirectory.gov.in/district.php

7. Amit tried selling his garments through electronic marketplaces but had to stop when the cost of returns and refunds exceeded what he could afford. It wasn't just that one in three pieces were returned—a higher volume than he expected—but that some buyers were clearly taking advantage of the return policy: The garments they sent back were visibly used.

8. Adapted from Amolo Ng'weno and David Porteous, 'Let's Be Real: The Informal Sector and the Gig Economy Are the Future, and the Present, of Work in Africa', Centre for Global Development, 2018. Available at: https://www.cgdev.org/publication/lets-be-real-informal-sector-and-gig-economy-are-future-and-present-work-africa

9. 'Impact of internet and digitisation on SMBs in India', KPMG India and Google, 2017. Available at: https://assets.kpmg/content/dam/kpmg/in/pdf/2017/01/Impact-of-internet-and-digitisation.pdf

10. David Eaves and Ben McGuire, 'Lessons from Estonia on digital government', *Policy Options Politiques*, 2019. Available at: https://policyoptions.irpp.org/magazines/february-2019/lessons-estonia-digital-government/

11. Information available to every government arm: Rainer Kattel and Ines Mergel, 'Estonia's Digital Transformation', University College London, 2018. Available at: https://www.ucl.ac.uk/bartlett/public-purpose/sites/public-purpose/files/iipp-wp-2018-09_estonias_digital_transformation.pdf

    800 years of working time: Heiko Vainsalu, 'How do Estonians save annually 820 years of work without much work?', e-Estonia, 2017. Available at: https://e-estonia.com/how-save-annually-820-years-of-work/

CHAPTER 33: SMALL BUSINESS, LARGE IMPACT

1. Based on analysis done by Tata Sons and Dalberg. India's total workforce is projected to increase from 454 million

in 2014 to 533 million by 2030. The baseline distribution of the workforce in 2030 is assumed to evolve (broadly) in line with historical trends. Farmers will decline as a share of the workforce. Similarly, the share of casual labourers, public administration and defence employees, and self-employed will also come down marginally. Concurrently, there will be an increase in the share of employment in the private sector, with firm sizes of 2–9, 10–199 and 200+ employees. However, it is assumed that the distribution within these three categories will remain the same in 2030, as in 2014.

For the everywhere entrepreneurship scenario, a further decline in casual labour and self-employment is modelled, while the number of farmers, government and defence employees continues to be the same as in the baseline scenario. We project SME employment—employment in 10–199 category—will increase to 30 per cent of private sector employment (self-employment and employment in firms with 2–9, 10–199 and 200+ employees), similar to developing country averages. The other categories are adjusted accordingly.

CHAPTER 34: NEW AIMS

1. Per capita income: 'Economic Survey of Karnataka 2017–18', Government of Karnataka, 2017–18. Available at: http://planning.kar.nic.in/docs/Economic%20Survey%20Reports/ES_17-18/English.pdf

Education and literacy statistics: 'District and State report cards', DISE, National Institute of Educational Planning and Administration, 2016–17. Available at: http://udise.in/ElementarySRC-2013-14.htm?ay=2016-17#

2. Based on analysis by Tata Sons and TCS. The extra doctor-hours are calculated based on an estimate that 50,000 oncology surgeries are performed every year at private and public hospitals across India.

CHAPTER 35: ASHAS

1. ASHAs—Accredited Social Health Activists—play a key role in the National Rural Health Mission, launched in 2005. As trained community health workers, selected from the village itself, they work as an interface between the community and the public health system. Their role includes creating awareness on health issues, mobilizing the community towards local health planning, and increasing utilization of the existing health services. Originally, they focused heavily on maternal and child health, but additional duties such as tuberculosis care and screening for non-communicable diseases have been added to their responsibilities. As of 2018, there are 1,023,136 ASHAs across the country. India's maternal mortality ratio has shown a decline to 167 per 100,000 live births in the period 2011–13 from 212 between 2007–09. The infant mortality rate has also seen a decline to 37 per 1,000 live births in 2015, from 42 in 2012. ASHAs are not the only reason for the decline, but multiple studies reinforce the importance of their role.

CHAPTER 37: UBAYAKUSHALAOPARI

1. Estimates show 53 per cent of women and 23 per cent of men in India aged 15–49 have anaemia. The prevalence of anaemia is consistently high, at more than 50 per cent, in almost all subgroups of women. Source: National Family Health Survey (NFHS-4), Ministry of Health and Family Welfare, 2015–16. Available at: http://rchiips.org/nfhs/NFHS-4Reports/India.pdf

CHAPTER 39: THE BRIDGITAL MODEL

1. For a more detailed methodology note, refer to the technical appendix of 'A Future That Works: Automation, Employment and Productivity', McKinsey Global Institute, January 2017. Available at : https://www.mckinsey.com/~/media/mckinsey/featured%20insights/Digital%20Disruption/Harnessing%20automation%20for%20a%20future%20that%20works/MGI-A-future-that-works-Executive-summary.ashx

2. The diagram shows that 25–30 per cent of doctor time is freed up through a combination of automation and the shifting of tasks. This is the outcome of an extensive piece of analysis using multiple sources: McKinsey Global Institute's Automation Model, expert interviews with McKinsey & Company's Healthcare Practice team, and time-motion studies across five private and public healthcare service delivery facilities. This estimate is generalized to the 'average doctor' given that a variety of doctors were surveyed, including specialists like

Notes

paediatricians, general surgeons, neonatologists, oncological surgeons, as well as general medicine doctors. This was done to average out differences in time use across medical specializations and types of facilities. For instance, compared to doctors in public health facilities, doctors in private health facilities often spend more time on core tasks, less time on administrative duties, and are more advanced adopters of digital technologies. The case of the oncological surgeon mentioned previously in the chapter is an example of this— the inefficiencies in time use were relatively high, given it took place in a public hospital with limited digitisation.

3. Estimations based on work by Tata Sons and McKinsey & Company. There is no ready estimate of the number of doctors in India. The figures reported in government data are based on the Medical Council of India's database of registered doctors. It includes the stock of all registered doctors starting from the 1960s, when the registry was begun, and hasn't been adjusted to reflect death, retirement, emigration or exit from the medical profession. We made adjustments using the methodology in Basant Potnuru, 'Aggregate availability of doctors in India: 2014-2030', *Indian Journal of Public Health*, 2017 to estimate practising doctors. This suggests applying an adjustment factor of 25–35 per cent to reported figures to account for doctors registered, but not available.

India currently has the capacity to train around 66,000 doctors per year. Most of the increase in capacity has been recent, and will only reflect 3–5 years from now. Net additions, adjusting for emigrations and retirement from

311

the existing stock of doctors, is estimated to be 30,000 per year before 2025, and rises to 50,000 per year after 2025. Incremental doctor addition to the stock of registered doctors is adjusted to reflect this increase—even though this assumes a much tighter link between the capacity for training doctors and the availability of doctors, than seen in practice.

4. Estimations based on work by Tata Sons and McKinsey & Company. We can think of doctors in the Bridgital healthcare system—the Bridgital doctors of the future—as capable of servicing more patients than doctors currently. In effect, this is equivalent to adding to the stock of doctors in the healthcare system. Freeing up doctor time via automation and task shifting provides the equivalent of an additional 286,116 doctors by 2025 and 372,710 doctors by 2030. This addresses more than 90 per cent of the gap to the normative level of one doctor per thousand population in 2030 (than would happen without the Bridgital intervention).

CHAPTER 40: BRIDGITAL MORE BROADLY

1. Formally extension services refer to the 'provision of information services to farmers'. Agriculture extension workers bridge the gap between farmers and the latest agricultural research. They do so by communicating market developments and new technologies to farmers, fostering linkages to markets and the agricultural value chain, and training in new skills to improve farmer livelihoods. The aim is to enhance farmers' knowledge about crop techniques and help them increase

their productivity. The forms of such engagement include training courses, farm trials and trade events, among others. The penetration of public extension services in India is low—estimated to be lower than 10 per cent of farmers in 2012. See 'Fact sheet on extension services', Global Forum for Rural Advisory Services, 2012. A 2011 study by M.J. Chandragowda found that over a third of the 140,000 extension worker positions in the Department of Agriculture remained vacant.

2. China and Vietnam have more than one public sector extension worker per village (one per 250–350 farm households or 0.8–0.9 villages). In Indonesia, one public sector extension worker covers around three villages. India has sanctioned positions for a span of seven villages, with vacancies worsening the ratio to one per eleven villages. The potential augmented extension workers is calculated assuming India achieves the levels of coverage of China and Vietnam in the high case, and the average of Indonesia, China and Vietnam in the low case, while also filling existing vacancies. sixty per cent of our projected 2025 farm holdings are assumed to adopt some form of Bridgital extension services. The number of farm holdings in 2025 is estimated based on the growth rate of 1.4 per cent per year, calculated for the last five-year period before the 2011 agricultural census.

3. McKinsey & Company analysis, based on interviews with multiple logistics start-ups.

4. Estimations based on work by Tata Sons and McKinsey & Company, as well as 'India's Trillion-Dollar Digital Economy', Government of India, Ministry of Electronics & Information Technology (MEITY), February 2019.

Index

315

Index

automation, 4–5, 38–49,
232–33
'Ayushman Bharat', 78, 240

Balwadis, 115
Bank of Tokyo-Mitsubishi
UFJ, Japan, 116
Barak Valley, Assam, 58
Bengaluru's start-ups, 197–99
Bhore Committee. *See* Health
Survey and Development
Committee
Breakthrough, an NGO,
124–25
Broker, Girija, 105-06
bureaucracy, 7, 19, 202–04,
205
Burman, Nikhil, 27–29,
30–33, 53–55, 59, 79, 226
business process outsourcing,
39

Cachar Cancer Hospital,
Silchar, 53, 65–67
cancer prevalence and
treatment, 54, 57–68
care centre, child care
economy, 113–17

professionalization of, 118
quality services, 118–19
stigma of outsourcing care,
117–18
care coordinators, 226–27
caste discrimination, 91, 99
Centre for Monitoring Indian
Economy, 96
child sex ratio, 107
childcare provision and
parental leave,
in India, 18, 120–22
in Japan, 116
in Mexico, 114-15
in Sweden, 114, 118, 122
China, 8, 35, 38, 42, 71, 96,
105, 137, 140, 243
Clinicograph, 219–22, 230
cloud-based management
system, 119
cognition, cognitive ability, 5,
114, 115, 232
collaboration, 43, 47, 126,
244–45, 249, 250
collective intervention, 48
community health workers,
215
computers, 36, 39, 253

Index

Index

Thailand, 71
trust, 68
Vietnam, 71
domestic markets, 8
dowry deaths, 90
drought, 2003, 145

ease of doing business, 84,
     188, 205
e-commerce, 128, 200
e-governance systems, 203, 205
economic and technology-led
     transitions, 4
economic development, 133,
     144
economic growth, India, 8,
     13, 56, 140, 156
     does not reflect job
          growth, 161–62, 168
economies of scale, 180
economy, India, 6, 8–9, 10,
     11, 13–14, 95–96, 142,
     150, 156–57, 161
     automation, 46, 233
     formal sector, 119, 143,
          149, 152
     human capital
          mismanagement, 155

informal sector, 10, 20,
     135, 142, 150, 164,
     179–80
     split nature, 47
education, education system,
     11, 15–16, 82–83, 150,
     153, 194, 244, 252,
     255
     based on five principles,
          249–50
     Bridgital approach, 239,
          240
     constraints, 134–36,
          165–67
     and employment testing,
          44
     informal, 173–75
     investment, 156
     outcomes and transitions,
          156
     low and inconsistent
          quality, 154
     tertiary education, 154,
          155
electricity, 40–41, 195, 253
electronic medical records, 79
employability, 16, 154, 251
employment, 13, 156, 162

Index

income per capita, 7–8

Indian Journal of Public
Health, 71

Indonesia: women's
representation in micro,
small and medium
enterprises (MSMEs),
127–28

industrial policies
Rwanda, 193–94
Singapore, 193
South Korea, 193

Industrial Revolution
Third, 39
Fourth, 4, 39–40, 42, 47,
250, 254

information technology (IT),
8, 39, 146, 197

innovation, 16, 48, 57, 185,
200, 202, 221–22, 249,
253, 255–56

integrated physical-digital
perspective, 42–45

intermediaries, 15

Internet of Things (IoT), 2,
14, 43

Jan Dhan Yojana, 35, 242

Japan, 8, 38, 156
care economy, 116, 118
policy, 120

job
and access, bridgital,
19–20
twin challenges, 9–14,
17–23, 208
challenge, 9–11, 97, 150,
168–69, 235
growth, 19, 161–62,
240–42
search, 141
security, 10

judicial system, judiciary,
India, 2, 12, 188, 256
Bridgital approach, 239,
242

Jugaad, tweaks and tricks, 64,
254

Kaku, Michio, 5

Kalyani Hospital, Silchar,
Assam, 29, 59–60, 62–65

Kolar, Karnataka, 208, 212,
213, 216, 218, 220, 223–
24, 228–29, 237

Kumar, Dr, 228–29

Index

Index